Praise for *Unruly Saint*

"When Dorothy Day walked this earth in the 1920s and '30s she witnessed a world much like our own—convulsing in a torrent of race riots, deep economic inequity, the cresting wave of women's suffrage, an America fighting to keep power in Protestant hands—all in the shadow of the trauma of the 1918 Influenza pandemic. In that context, Day's Catholic Worker movement lit a prophetic fire that changed the world. In an age when followers of Jesus are navigating similar headlines, Day's life witness stands tall among giants. D.L. Mayfield's *Unruly Saint* is a gift to the church and to the world for right now."

—**Lisa Sharon Harper**, author, and founder and president of Freedom Road

"In *Unruly Saint*, D.L. Mayfield shares a consequential and captivating story that I could not put down. Her style is moving, revealing, and vulnerable. I imagine Dorothy Day herself is looking down and smiling."

—**Randy S. Woodley**, author, activist, and co-sustainer at Eloheh Indigenous Center for Earth Justice

"In *Unruly Saint*, D.L. Mayfield offers what she says is her 'personal engagement with the life of Dorothy Day.' More than forty years after Day's death and as her cause for sainthood is being considered at the Vatican, everyone who speaks or writes about her reveals their personal engagement (or lack of it) with Day's life, whether they intend this or not. Mayfield comes to her book, she says, 'as a mother, a daughter, a sometimes activist, an anxious neighbor, and a very lonely and religious soul,' and her telling of Day's life is all the more impelling for it."

—**Brian Terrell**, activist and longtime Catholic Worker

"The danger of our relationship to saints is that all too often, we strip away their humanity and reduce them to pious statuettes. In *Unruly Saint*, D.L. Mayfield enfleshes the least likely of American saints, Dorothy Day, infusing this often-misunderstood figure with lively, thoughtful prose. In a time when church leaders try to remake Dorothy Day's story in light of their own wants and needs, Mayfield's book instead asks us to meet a flawed but holy Dorothy Day pulsing with human life. A necessary book for our time, *Unruly Saint* will introduce many readers to Dorothy Day and deepen many others' relationship to her."

—**Kaya Oakes**, journalist, teacher, and author of *The Defiant Middle: How Women Claim Life's In-Betweens to Remake the World*

"In *Unruly Saint*, D.L. Mayfield does more than trace the life of Dorothy Day as a social justice activist, disruptor of the status quo, and friend to the poor. This work rekindles the hope that we can live with integrity, serve others, and do it all in the name of a Savior who modeled the same. Read this book to be challenged, inspired, and connected to a historic faith that can help change the world for good."

—**Jemar Tisby, PhD**, *New York Times*–bestselling author of *The Color of Compromise* and *How to Fight Racism*

"*Unruly Saint* is a book for those who have never quite known what to do with Dorothy Day, or perhaps what to do with themselves. Just as D.L. Mayfield finds in Day a friend and guide who meets her in her own spiritual loneliness, this book invites readers into that friendship, into a community forged through justice and love. Like Day, Mayfield 'carries a lantern for us lonely souls in our current chaotic and confusing time.' Winsome, earnest, and disruptive, *Unruly Saint* is a delightfully provocative read."

—**Kristin Kobes Du Mez**, historian and author of
Jesus and John Wayne

"Few people have impacted me more than Dorothy Day. Actually, few people have impacted the church in the twentieth century more than Day, even though her name is still unfamiliar to many. That's why I'm so pumped about this new book by my friend D.L. Mayfield. *Unruly Saint* beautifully captures the spirit of Dorothy Day in all its candor, grunge, and messiness. Day's message is prophetically on point today, just as it was fifty years ago. Enough theologizing and pontificating. Enough political rhetoric and virtual activism. This book is about revolution, but it's also about doing dishes and weeding the garden."

—**Shane Claiborne**, author, activist, and cofounder
of Red Letter Christians

"Far from the familiar whitewashed image of a conservative pious do-gooder, D.L. Mayfield brings to life the radical Catholic anarchist who is Dorothy Day. Mayfield beautifully illustrates Day's passion for serving and empowering the poor and revives the vision we need to continue Day's work of building a new world. This book is a gift to everyone who needs a radical friend, like Day, to inspire us to put our faith into action."

—**Damon Garcia**, author of *The God Who Riots*

"Roiled with the Great Influenza pandemic, the Great Depression, and the burgeoning wave of fascism, the times of Dorothy Day mirror our own. Her life illustrates what faithfulness looks like in troubled times. D.L. Mayfield reveals the heart, energy, and direction of this unruly but utterly human saint as she writes Day's story with a depth of admiration and evident affection. Not only that, you can feel the kinship between these two women, separated by time but aligned in gospel purpose and spirited passion for God's good news to the poor. Together they stretch our current imagination, showing what is possible when we take the Sermon on the Mount seriously in times of poverty, pandemic, and political upheaval."

—**Kelley Nikondeha**, author of *The First Advent in Palestine: Reversals, Resistance, and the Ongoing Complexity of Hope*

"D.L. Mayfield has written a book about Dorothy Day that Day herself would be happy with because it takes the questions about faith and society that Day lived seriously enough to ask them of ourselves in this moment. *Unruly Saint* is neither a biography nor a memoir, but a unique confession that invites us to walk with Day, Mayfield, God, and the poor toward beloved community."

—**Jonathan Wilson-Hartgrove**, author of *Revolution of Values*

"Avoiding the easy, wide road of a triumphant hero's journey, *Unruly Saint* takes the rare, narrow path of unflinchingly honest storytelling. The result is an absolute marvel of a book that confronts the muck of injustice with the stubborn belief that another world is possible. A sorely needed story for our times, and it's hard to think of a better person to tell it."

—**Peter Choi**, author of *George Whitefield: Evangelist for God and Empire* and director of the Faith and Justice Network

"Grace Lee Boggs always asked, 'What time is it on the clock of the world?' These days, answering that question leads to uncontrollable rage or unceasing weeping. How do we face this moment with courage? Is it even possible to make space for beauty and delight? Through our weariness, so many of us hunger for elders and ancestors to walk beside us and prod our hearts and imagination. Dorothy Day is one such companion who beckons us to come and sit around the table, trusting the sacred conspiring born of community. Mayfield writes that if more of us took Dorothy Day seriously, 'the disruption to society would be immediate and overwhelming.' Read this book, and may it be so."

—**Lydia Wylie-Kellermann**, editor of *Geez* magazine and *The Sandbox Revolution*

"We have a tendency to place our holy heroes into tidy boxes—restricting their lives to a vision, a mission, and an effortless perfection. Because of that, the saints and blessed ones and servants of God meant to accompany us along our faith journey often feel out of our reach. In reality, each of their lives was so much more complicated than that tidy box. In her book *Unruly Saint*, D.L. Mayfield breaks the box open for one of our most important modern holy heroes: Dorothy Day. Day's story—her faith and her activism—has impacted untold numbers around the world and has the potential to impact infinitely more. But only if we resist the urge to confine her to that tidy box. With this book, Mayfield sets the tone for all of us to remember Day as she was—a person who should leave us feeling comforted and unsettled—and for that, I'll always be grateful."

—**Tommy Tighe**, author of *St. Dymphna's Playbook*

"There are few women who have impacted my life the way Dorothy Day has, and there are equally few people whom I would trust to write about her. D.L. Mayfield is one of those people. With evident love and a curious spirit, Mayfield resurrects this dynamo just when we need her the most. This book is as honest and relentless as Day herself."

—**Shannon K. Evans**, author of *Rewilding Motherhood: Your Path to an Empowered Feminine Spirituality*

"Dorothy Day has always fit uncomfortably in the weird world of American Christianity. As the cause for her canonization accelerates, D.L. Mayfield offers a full portrait of Day's radical witness to a God of the poor, embracing the contradictions and promise of her life for Christians in the twenty-first century."

—**Dean Dettloff**, cohost of *The Magnificast* and section editor for *Geez* magazine

UNRULY SAINT

UNRULY SAINT

DOROTHY DAY'S RADICAL VISION AND
ITS CHALLENGE FOR OUR TIMES

D.L. MAYFIELD

 Broadleaf Books

Minneapolis

To Ramona and Ransom,
my two miracles

CONTENTS

AUTHOR'S NOTE

There are many excellent biographies of Dorothy Day already written. This book does not claim to be one of them. Instead, it is my personal engagement with the life of Dorothy Day in the years surrounding the birth of the Catholic Worker movement. I come to this book as a mother, a daughter, a sometimes activist, an anxious neighbor, and a very lonely and religious soul. I come to this book as a friend of Dorothy's, as much as I can be, separated by time and history.

It is not a hagiography nor a memoir; it is instead as true of an account as I could write, trying to pay attention to this remarkable woman. I love her very much, and she has been a companion to me as I have journeyed through some of the questions around how to be a person of faith in an unequal and unjust world. In many ways, it is a story about the birth of a movement—the problems of the world, a group of people who come together to address those issues, the heady early years, and the questions and growing pains as life continues.

I am not a Catholic, historian, or biographer. I am somebody trying very hard to pay attention to the ways that God is at work in the world. I am somebody who has felt the long loneliness and who has been both unsettled and comforted by the life and words of Dorothy Day. She remains as relevant today as she was in the 1930s, and there is something both troubling and healing about this fact. Her relevance is an indictment of how little has changed in our rotten political and social systems, even as her faithfulness is lauded as a symbol of how to move forward in a world where we have forgotten how to love our neighbors as ourselves.

Still, *little by little*, she would say near the end of her life. Little by little, we love God by loving each other. And this book is one of my little ways of trying to love both God and Dorothy, our unjust world, and all the beautiful people in it.

ROBERT ELLSBERG

When Pope Francis spoke to Congress in 2015, he included Dorothy Day on a shortlist of four "great Americans," beginning with Abraham Lincoln. I find it notable, for someone who pursued such a consequential vocation, that until the age of thirty-five she had absolutely no idea of what she was meant to do with her life.

Not that her prior life had been uneventful. She had dropped out of college, worked as a muckraking journalist, joined with fellow radicals in the struggle for a just world, hung out in speakeasies with famous poets and playwrights, twice gone to jail, worked as a nurse, fallen in love, experienced heartache, and twice—apparently—tried to commit suicide. And that was just the beginning. She also wrote a novel, fell in love again, gave birth to a daughter, made the astonishing leap to become a Catholic, and set off on the lonely path of a single mother. But she still, as Bono would say, hadn't found what she was looking for.

She was looking for a way to combine her newfound faith with her commitment to the poor and oppressed. And then, after issuing a heartfelt prayer "with tears and anguish," she met Peter Maurin, a holy philosopher-hobo from France, who urged her to start a movement to promote the radical social message of the gospel. It would begin with a newspaper launched on May 1, 1933, and then a house of hospitality to practice the works of mercy, and then maybe farming communes, and then . . . who could say? The important thing was to start today, where they were, to take the first step, to begin "building a new world in the shell of the old."

Dorothy's life before that encounter was dry kindling in search of a spark. Peter Maurin provided that spark and thereby set Dorothy on a path of revolutionary love-in-action and spiritual adventure. What I love about D.L. Mayfield's book is that she is interested in the story of that spark and she brings to Dorothy's story her own yearning and readiness for something new.

Dorothy died over forty years ago, and most of those who knew her remember her from her old age. I include myself, having made my way to the Catholic Worker Movement in 1975 at the age of nineteen and stayed on for five years until just before her death in 1980. Although she was bent with age, hard of hearing, and, ultimately, unable to leave her room, my deepest sense of Dorothy was her surprising youthfulness. She identified with young people, their passions, their searching, and their "instinct for the heroic." She took us seriously, listening to our opinions, trusting us to make our own mistakes and learn from them, always encouraging us to believe—regardless of what the world might say—that we could change ourselves and change the world.

She would love D.L. and her own passionate and questing spirit. D.L.'s account would surely take her back to so many scenes from the early days, when she and her companions set out to invent something new, a new way of following Christ, a new way of holiness, a new way of setting the world on fire. As Dorothy wrote at the end of her memoir, *The Long Loneliness*, "It all happened as we sat there talking, and it is still going on."

In her encounter with Dorothy, D.L. has caught that spark. And in this book, she passes it on.

Lent 2022

Robert Ellsberg

Robert Ellsberg is publisher of Orbis Books, former managing editor of *The Catholic Worker*, and editor of five volumes of Dorothy Day's writings, including her diaries and her selected letters.

INTRODUCTION

Writing a book is hard, because you are giving
yourself away. But if you love,
you want to give yourself.

—**Dorothy Day**, *The Long Loneliness*

I n 2015, Pope Francis visited the United States and gave a historic address to the members of Congress. When he expressed gratitude about being invited to speak in "the land of the free and the home of the brave," he received a standing ovation from the crowd of politicians and journalists in Washington, DC. Francis, originally from Argentina, spoke about the spiritual and moral legacy of the United States and the need for work to continue in the areas of poverty, the abolition of the death penalty, and addressing the global refugee crisis, among other issues. He also highlighted four exemplars from US history, great people of faith who moved America's moral and social imagination forward in distinct ways.

As Pope Francis talked about Abraham Lincoln, Martin Luther King Jr., and Thomas Merton, heads nodded around the room—all familiar names in the story of America that we tell ourselves.

Then he mentioned Dorothy Day, and journalists began frantically typing into search engines on their smart phones and computers, all asking the same question: who the heck is Dorothy Day?

Kate Hennessy, Dorothy Day's granddaughter, laughs as she tells this beloved story: In comparison with the three men Francis mentioned, Dorothy Day is the least well-known figure in popular culture. Yet to Francis, and to many other people both Catholic and non-Catholic, Dorothy Day is one of the most important figures in the American twentieth century.

When she died over forty years ago in 1980, the news made the front page of the *New York Times*. Her obituary described her legacy of engaging Catholics and people of faith in the work of social justice through the newspaper she founded, her "houses of hospitality," and her "luminous" personality. It was all written about breathlessly: her communist background, her love of the poor, and her desire to see people of faith at the forefront of social justice issues. From the obituary, it was clear she was the kind of paradox that intrigues the world.

Famously leftist in her ideals, she also loved the traditions and liturgy of Roman Catholicism. When she publicly clashed with church authority figures throughout her life, people near her remained mystified that she wasn't denounced or excommunicated. Perhaps, mused the writer of her *New York Times* obituary, it was because the cardinals themselves suspected they might be dealing with a saint. A stubborn, smiling, unruly saint who never stopped seeing the face of Christ in the faces of the poor around her. And anyone she came into contact with, she invited to do the same.

Forty years after her death, her vision for what it looks like to be a person of faith in tumultuous times is more relevant than ever. Dorothy Day was a trailblazer, a curmudgeon, deeply radical and deeply drawn to religious and cultural traditions. In the US halls of power, Pope Francis commended her as an exemplary American, one to strive to be like. He said this while surely knowing Dorothy Day was once considered a person of interest by the FBI (complete with extensive file on her), knowing she publicly encouraged people to resist conscription into any war effort, knowing she was arrested numerous times in her life, and that she was a proud federal tax resistor.[1]

The irony of Pope Francis praising Dorothy Day—a thorn in the side of the US government—not despite her faith but precisely because of it is not lost on me. As I watched the pope speak to Congress on the screen, I wondered if the people gathered that day knew the significance of Dorothy Day being upheld as an American saint, someone who shines a light on the way forward in the United States. She is and was a complex woman, and even more importantly, if even a few of us started to live our lives more like her, the disruption to society would be immediate and overwhelming. The world would turn upside down. A revolution of the heart, of our economics and politics, would be enacted. And it would be expressly at odds with the deals being brokered in the halls of Congress.

Who the heck is Dorothy Day? I like to think about the journalists and politicians frantically searching for information on her, who were unprepared for what her life and her story might one day ask of them. Perhaps you have heard snippets about this woman, champion of the poor, and the jewel of Catholic social thought in the twentieth century. Maybe that is what brought you here. I know it's what brought me to write this book, bringing my own personal questions and interests into her life and story, trying to answer those questions for a new audience and generation, trying to answer them for myself—because God knows I need an unruly saint to journey with in these trying times. And maybe you need an unruly saint as well.

I discovered Dorothy Day in the thick of a personal crisis moment. I had been raised in the white Evangelical Church in the United States, had tried hard to be a very good Christian, and spent a few years as a young woman trying to convert some of my neighbors— newly arrived refugees from Somalia—like any good missionary would. But instead of converting anyone, I was overwhelmed with the lived realities of my neighbors, who were poor and marginalized in America.

My religious platitudes shriveled on my lips. I realized all the content I had learned from my Bible college professors and textbooks had nothing to say to these neighbors struggling to buy food and pay rent in my city, in my country—a place I had always been told was good news for those who only worked hard enough. The inequality and the gap between the rich and the poor astonished me and struck me as deeply antithetical to how God wanted the world to be.

I continued to try to follow the rules for being a good religious person. But when I went out to share the gospel, I found a world of people who had worked very, very hard and still had lives full of pain and suffering. These new friends and neighbors would listen politely, nodding their heads as I would try to talk about Jesus coming to earth and dying for their sins, and then they'd ask me for help reading their pile of bills, which continued to grow on their countertops. They dealt with rat and cockroach infestations, greedy landlords, and the ever-present fear of evictions. They had family members in faraway countries constantly reaching out with news of death and suffering and pleas for help. On their tables were credit cards with 30 percent interest rates, and outside their doors, these Muslim neighbors met with hate crimes against them. In their low-income neighborhoods, there were no parks or grocery stores within walking distance. Their public schools were understaffed and under-resourced. The barriers to thriving added up wherever I started to look.

I slowly began to see small glimpses into the systemic inequality built into my world and wondered if it was on purpose. It sobered me and all of my memorized religious answers right up. I saw how difficult it was to thrive in my country for people who weren't white, college-educated, English-speaking, and Christian with middle-class families and support systems to fall back on— just like me.

Beyond being shocked by inequality and injustice in the United States, I was in spiritual crisis as well. What would Jesus say to people barely scraping by in an unjust system? Later, I would find voices like Howard Thurman, whose experience growing up the grandson of enslaved people in the United States caused him to be on a lifelong quest to ask what the Christian religion meant for the disinherited people of the world—those who had their backs to the wall. At this time in my life, I didn't know anyone else even asking this question, because I had been raised in a religious environment where people had privilege and power and where Christianity was intermixed with upholding the status quo. As an idealistic young woman, my sense of loneliness and dismay grew ever deeper. I was also confused. I had been explicitly taught I would be the saintly one walking into low-income apartments with my Bible in hand. I had been told I would bring God with me into places where God was not present. But, instead, I met with the opposite.

I was being invited to sit down on couches and eat meals cooked over a stove for hours on end, invited to experience the face of Christ in the apartments of friends who had been resettled from far-flung and war-torn countries. I met Jesus in their hand-shakes, hugs, and kisses on my cheek; in the apartment doors left open a crack for me to come in and sit down; the meals of rice and beans and curry and stew; the waving of a hand to sit down and watch a grainy VHS of a wedding of a distant relative in Texas or Tanzania or Afghanistan.

I didn't bring Christ anywhere: instead, I found him every-where in cockroach-infested apartments on the very outer edge of my city. The image of the invisible God in every single one of my new-to-me neighbors. I was made to feel welcome even as my eyes opened to new realities of sin and injustice all around.

The saddest part of being an evangelical Christian was that I was so trained to see myself as the savior that I had absolutely no language for the miracles I was experiencing. There was no one with whom I could even process this without being viewed as either a failure or a heretic. I was lost and overwhelmed, and I felt increasingly isolated from my Christian community.

It was at this moment I first encountered Dorothy Day. At an event for social justice Christian types, I was given a pin that said "If you have two coats, you have stolen one from the poor," a quote attributed to someone named Dorothy Day. Electrified by that phrase, I thought immediately of my refugee neighbors, their lack of material possessions, and the juxtaposition of all the other people I knew with closets stuffed full of clothes. (I also felt quite smug since at that point in my life I did indeed only own one coat.)

This simple quote of Dorothy's (which she got from her friend Peter Maurin, who got it from St. Basil, who got it from John the Baptist) highlighted the inequality in our world while pointing me toward a God who would not rest until all were taken care of. It was both comforting and damning, a double-edged sword, a mixture I have come to associate more and more with the life and spirituality of Dorothy Day.

I bought and began to read her autobiography, *The Long Loneliness*, thrilled by every new bit of information I gleaned about this radical woman. Only a few years into my reading, I was already discovering how incredibly isolating and exhausting it was to try to change the world by the sheer force of my goodwill. The troubles were too great, and I didn't see the Christians around me helping in practical ways the people who were barely making it in our city. Disillusionment creeping in, filled with the idealism and smugness of youth, I slowly started to read about this woman who stubbornly refused to believe we should be content with the world as it is. I read about her love of God impossibly mixed up with her fierce love for her neighbors and a desire to see a better world for them here and now. As I read, I hoped with all of my sad and earnest little heart that this intense woman and her views on God would make me feel a little less lonely as I tried to navigate our beautiful, broken world.

And she has done just that—she's become a trusted companion and a friend, as the best writers can be. But more than that, Dorothy has become to me an unsettling force: a pebble in my shoe, a ripple in my serene pond. She's a stumbling block for those who want a happy life free of responsibilities to their neighbor, to people who want to love Jesus without living like him. For me, she's been a wonderful and annoying saint. But she certainly hasn't made my life any easier—and a part of me knows she would be terribly pleased by this.

"We have all known the long loneliness," Dorothy Day wrote in 1952, "and the only cure is community." Dorothy titled her bestselling autobiography *The Long Loneliness* in part because she was inspired by her daughter, Tamar, who wrote a letter about the loneliness of being home and mothering multiple small children. This phrase reminded Dorothy of a quote from the nun Mary Ward, who said that following God leads to great pain, but that it is endurable.[2] *The Long Loneliness* is how Dorothy chose to describe her own life and the lives of the people she loved the most. The phrase came to her mind again as she wrote about the death of her friend and mentor and the cofounder of the Catholic Worker movement, Peter Maurin. As he became quiet and withdrawn in the last five years of his life, he felt lost in the world that he had tried for so many years to change. She thought of the endless revolving door of the desperate poor she sought to help and the do-gooders who came and stayed for weeks, months, a few years and then left to pursue other lives. She remembered the saints she was so drawn to, both the ecstasy of being close to God and their loneliness and times of inward struggle. In her writings, letters, and diaries, these themes were always present—the delight of being alive and the crushing weight of living in a world full of suffering.

As I write this, we are over one hundred years removed from the turn of the twenty-first century that shaped Dorothy Day— the heady idealism of the radicals of the time, the disillusionment over the first great war, the horrific influenza of 1918, the Roaring Twenties, and the subsequent Great Depression. Born at the cusp of centuries, in 1898, Dorothy was a young woman in the thick of the convergence of these ideals and events, times of social change and political movements. Her first great passions were politics, labor causes, and being a literary artist. She made friends with people influential in socialist, literary, and artistic communities in both Chicago and New York. She frequented seedy bars and interviewed famous Russian politicians and lived the life of a liberated woman long before that was anywhere near the norm. In 1927, she became a Catholic and brought together her faith with an understanding of political systems and profound concern for the poor. Five years later, she met Peter Maurin and started the *Catholic Worker* newspaper, which launched a movement of Catholic social thought and action that continues to this day.

Now, almost a century later, she is admired by popes and talked about in the halls of Congress; she is on her way to being canonized a saint of the Catholic Church (a cause still in process), while hundreds of thousands already treat her as one. According to different folks, Dorothy Day is an exemplary American, a luminous Catholic, a divisive figure, a radical leftist, a communist in disguise, a conservative defender of morality, a dangerous woman, a disgrace, a saint.

In all the years of her life, she was hard to quantify and categorize, and she liked this about herself. When, late in her life, her friend Robert Ellsberg requested a copy of the FBI file on her and read sections aloud to her—specifically how J. Edgar Hoover called her a threat to America—she remarked that the US government made her sound "like a mean old woman." She paused, thinking for a minute and smiling. Then she told Robert, "Read it to me again."

I view Dorothy Day as a woman who carries a lantern for us lonely souls in our current chaotic and confusing time. Her own inner light was nourished by so many odd and beautiful things: the Christ faces of the men lining the streets of the Bowery; a cup of coffee and a cigarette; her own daughter's face and laugh; a good Russian novel; beautiful music; the stories of the saints; the seaside; an electric night of conversation with socialists and communists, playwrights and drunks. All of these fed that inner burning, that conviction she held that God was good, God was love, and that God wanted people of the church to do something about the suffering of their fellow neighbors. Her burning heart illuminated something within me when I first read her autobiography several years ago. And when I continue to read and reflect on her writings, the fire gets fanned over and over again.

Pope Francis tried to tell the people in power about Dorothy Day. I'm not sure how many listened to him. He is someone whose own heart has been sparked by her life and who knows how much it would have made her laugh to be offered up as an exemplary American citizen. Enemy-of-the-state Dorothy Day, an American to be idealized? Not exactly. She told her friend Robert all those years ago, "When they call you a saint, basically it means that you are not to be taken seriously." I promise very little about this book, but I do promise one thing: I aim to take Dorothy and her life very seriously. I offer this reflection on her early life and years simply as her torch, held high, continues to shine. Perhaps you will be burned by it as well. Dorothy's story is one of perpetual conversions. Here are just a few of them shared in the hopes that they might spark some changes in all of us.

PART 1

—

THE BEGINNING YEARS

OUR LADY OF PERPETUAL CONVERSIONS

It's a difficult job to dip into the past, but it must be done. . . . I will try to trace for you the steps by which I came to accept the faith that I believe was always in my heart. For this reason, most of the time I will speak of the good I encountered even amid surroundings and people who tried to reject God.[1]

—**Dorothy Day**, *From Union Square to Rome*

When Dorothy Day converted to Catholicism at the age of thirty, her friends and family were shocked. Betrayed, even, dismayed and possibly slightly bemused. *Their Dorothy?* The woman who cut her hair into a short bob and smoked like a chimney and swore constantly and who was always going on and on about labor unions? *That Dorothy?* The one who had been writing and working for leftist papers, who was furiously impatient with all that was wrong in the world, the woman who did what she wanted when she wanted? The pregnant-out-of-wedlock free spirit who could quote Marx with the best of them and was always ready with a sarcastic retort or a girlish giggle? *That Dorothy Day had converted to Catholicism?*

Conversion narratives can be prone to flattening in their retelling, made shiny by constant repetition. They have a pattern to be followed: a life of chaos and sin before conversion and then a beautiful life of faith and trust with God after. A distinct and clear line that separates the "before" person and the "after" convert. But the truth of conversion, Dorothy knew, is that it is a lifelong process and that it never fully ends. It is both exhausting and liberating to realize this. When Dorothy tried to explain to her loved ones why she was now Catholic, she wanted to honor their questions and even their hurt. Would she be like the other religious folks and demean them and their yearnings for a better world? Would she forget about the struggle for equality and rights? Would she disappear into the halls of the Vatican, into the safe and comfortable pews of the local stained-glass church? Would she be content to pray for the evils of the world instead of picketing the companies that exploited their workers?

Not at all, Dorothy said. She aimed to convince her confused friends and the rest of the world that her conversion to the church would keep her more engaged in the struggle for a better world, not less. She knew her greatest gifts were her keen eyes and her curiosity about the world and her responsibility to others in it. So when she wrote down her conversion story, she made it plain that

God was with her in all the threads of her life, in all the tragedies and exultations, her yearning to be close to people in poverty and her urging others to change the world as soon as possible. In her stretching out her hands toward love, in her being overwhelmed by the cares of the world.

Why Catholicism, Dorothy? This must have been the question she got asked more than any other when she was in her thirties. Her eyes sharp and piercing, her mouth always ready to laugh at a good joke, her brain bursting with questions and insights into the issues of injustice and poverty and evil in the world. Why did she join the opiate of the masses that she had protested against for so long? It was a painful process for Dorothy to try to answer that question, and it took her many years and hundreds of paragraphs to get there. She wanted to honor the doubts and concerns of her closest comrades in the fight for justice as she slowly unspooled the truth about how captured she was by her love for God and how tired she was of keeping that hidden.

This was how Dorothy framed the beginning of her conversion story: It was radicals who loved the poor who pushed her toward God—eventually to the point where she had to break ranks with them and enter the Catholic Church. She grew up longing for the Divine and as a child would go to an Episcopal church with friends, where she would take in every element of the rituals, sights, and sounds—the cool, delicious feeling of reading the psalms and the liturgy, and the singing burrowing into her heart. Why did it feel like home to her?

Her parents were lapsed Episcopalians, so Dorothy was left to notice these impulses on her own. Like many intensely curious people, her questions started for her early in life. Even as a child, she said, she was aware of two things: First, how broken the world was and how it was filled with inequality and injustice. Second, she was aware of a longing for beauty and truth and joy that would randomly stop her in her tracks—what she came to call an encounter with the love of God. As a small girl, she was forever whispering thanks to God when she was happy, although no one taught her to do this. It burst forth out of her at her happiest moments, *thank you, thank you, thank you.*

But the older she got, the more disillusioned she became with the people who claimed to follow God. She would read the New Testament as a young teenager and be thrilled by Jesus in the gospels but quickly became disillusioned by organized religion. She said, "I distrusted all churches after reading the books of London and Sinclair," who pointed out societal evils and the lack of response by Christians. She loved reading about the saints who wanted to help the poor but felt troubled in her soul as the stories focused on personal piety and individual charity. To her, growing up in the middle of Chicago, seeing Polish immigrants worked to the bone for little pay and no reward, the issue seemed clear as day: "Why was so much done in remedying social evils instead of avoiding them in the first place? Where were the saints to try and change the social order, not just to minister to the slaves but to do away with slavery?"[2] Her youthfulness and her direct personality led her to see the hypocrisies of religion early on: "Children look at things very directly and simply. I did not see anyone taking off his coat and giving it to the poor. I didn't see anyone having a banquet and inviting in the lame, the halt, and the blind. And those who were doing it, like the Salvation Army, did not appeal to me. I wanted, though I did not know it then, a synthesis. I wanted life and I wanted the abundant life. I wanted it for others too."[3]

By the time she was seventeen and in her first year of college, starting to make friends with progressives and radicals, Dorothy made a conscious decision to dismiss Christianity entirely. The joy she had found in religious imagery and music and art as a child now horrified her: "Now that same happiness seemed to be a smug disregard of the misery of the world, a self-satisfied consciousness of being saved."[4]

As Dorothy saw it, the majority of Christians she knew used their religion to keep them safely ensconced away from the troubles of the world. They prayed their prayers and went to church and were confident they would get into heaven. Dorothy saw that for most of these people, changing the world order was not their priority because they benefited in so many ways from the unjust and unequal systems. She felt she must give up her religion in order to care about people, so she did.

Within the stories of people irrepressibly drawn to God is often a sense of mystery. Dorothy explored this in her writings, constantly pointing out how God found her in a variety of ways, including through communist, Marxist, and socialist friends just as much as through the words of her beloved Dostoevsky and Tolstoy or through the snatches of Christianity she caught by attending religious services as a child. All of it impacted Dorothy. Her conscience was primarily awakened and nourished by people vilified in dominant culture spaces: leftists, socialists, and those who were impacted by unemployment, houselessness, addiction, mental illness, and poverty.

A truly liberated woman, she committed herself to what she understood was a flawed institution and to a life of service. But that didn't mean she was done converting herself or others. No, she had her whole life to keep trying, and failing, and trying again. To point out the evils in society and to say thanks to God for whatever bit of goodness she could find. She wanted to do both, all the time. She wanted to be fully who she was, without apology. And so she entered the Catholic Church, bringing her whole self with her— much to the chagrin of nearly everyone in her life.

A truly free woman is hard to reckon with, both then and now. Which, to me, makes Dorothy's desire to live a life that allowed her to be a fully religious person and someone who longed to see the social order change all the more important. For the rest of her life, people wondered why she converted and then wondered why she stayed. She stayed because she found a community of people— in history, theology, and the streets of New York City—who also wanted to change the world. She stayed because of the Catholic Worker.

Dorothy tried to tell all of this to her friends as she wrote it down in her book, a collection of letters addressed to her brother John. I also took those letters as somehow written to me, giving me permission to see a future where Christianity was still possible for me, my family, and my neighborhood. She was trying to convince her radical friends, and in turn she influenced me.

But perhaps Dorothy really wrote the letters as a missive to both her younger and future selves, a testimony to the idea that we are always converting to something. She wanted the world to convert to be more like Christ, no matter what that might mean for her, and up until her death at age eighty-three, she continued to seek out a life of humility, repentance, and conversion through the lives and testimonies of her neighbors.

As I read and immersed myself in the ways Dorothy chose to tell the story of her conversion to the Catholic Church, I couldn't help but think, *If she is to be remembered as a saint, I think she would like to be known as one of perpetual conversion.*

MUCKRAKERS

Jesus said "blessed are the meek," but I could not be meek at the thought of injustice.

—Dorothy Day, *The Long Loneliness*

When Dorothy Day was fourteen years old, bright-eyed and inquisitive, the sheltered child of a lower-middle-class family in Chicago, she would walk the city, pushing her infant brother in a pram. Their mother, Grace, had difficulty recovering from the birth of her fifth, and last, child, and Dorothy became something of a surrogate mother to John. As a young teenager, she shouldered the burdens of her brother's care and possessively called him her baby. She would wake up at four in the morning to feed him his bottle of milk and take him on long walks through the Chicago streets after school during the witching hour, the times of fussing. She pushed the pram and walked the streets of the slums and the parks and affluent neighborhoods and started to pay attention to how it was all so close together. On these walks, Dorothy started to really see her city and get a sense for the inequality, suffering, and poverty that characterized wide swaths of it.

Her restless and intelligent eyes noticed it all, but she had few avenues to process what she was seeing. At night, after John was asleep, she would put together a plate of apples from the pantry and settle into a cozy chair in the living room. Curled up with one of the few books allowed into her home by her father, she would peel the apples one by one and eat them, searching her beloved books for answers to how the world worked.

One of the books she got her hands on was *The Jungle* by Upton Sinclair. In researching the book in 1905, Sinclair spent several months in the stockyards of Chicago interviewing the laborers—many of whom were recent immigrants from Eastern Europe—who were desperately trying to get a piece of the American dream at the turn of the century. Sinclair's novel tied history into his careful reporting of what he saw on the ground—he considered himself among the "muckrakers," or journalists seeking to shine a spotlight on the evils of the world in order to change it. *The Jungle* focused on the exploitative forces surrounding laborers in the meat-packing district of Chicago and ended with a plea for socialism as a better political structure than what he considered the unchecked and cruel capitalist system. Sinclair aimed at changing labor laws and protecting immigrant workers, raising the public consciousness, and horrifying readers into demanding the end of slave wages in the meat industry. And he wanted to inspire these changes through his fiction.

When Sinclair's novel became a smash hit in the publishing world, he was thrilled. But instead of it sparking a movement of fair wages for laborers as he hoped, *The Jungle* did something else—by encouraging President Roosevelt to investigate the book's claims, the US government enacted oversight and regulation of the food industry for the first time. Instead of changing the social order, capitalism continued on, now with more protections for the consumer goods people bought and ate. Sinclair despaired that his readers had missed the entire point of his novel. "I aimed at the public's heart and by accident I hit it in the stomach," he bemoaned.[1] His readers were horrified by the depictions of disease, filth, and rot in the meat being packaged for consumers but didn't see the lives and conditions of the humans who worked in these factories as worthy of protections.

Young Dorothy Day, however, was Sinclair's ideal reader. As she read the novel after a long afternoon walking in the city, *The Jungle* unveiled the truth of the horrors she saw in nearby neighborhoods. Past the green parks and her family's somewhat comfortable yet crowded life, there lived so many people just outside of her own experience, struggling to survive in an economic system that did not care about them beyond what could be squeezed out of their labor.

As she read, her route changed. She started walking east toward the meat-packing district and imagined the lives of the people she saw living and working in drab, awful conditions. Reading *The Jungle* was one of the first steps in her own journey of looking squarely at the injustice in the world and asking herself how she could be a part of making it just the tiniest bit better.

Much of her writing would center around the same themes that interested Sinclair: chronicling the lives of people in poverty, humanizing marginalized and exploited communities, demanding justice for laborers and more equitable laws, and aiming for hearts to change toward love and a new social order.

Muckrakers, those writers who tried to change the world for the better by exposing the muck of where it went wrong, attached themselves early on to Dorothy's heart. In her teen years, when she excelled in her local high school and devoured what social commentaries she could find, she also cooked and cleaned and took care of her siblings, walking the streets of her neighborhood and dreaming about all the mysteries it contained. Step by step, she was building up a worldview that connected with all the parts of her: her maternal side, her muckraking side, and her longing for a better world—one beyond her wildest dreams. She began to ask the questions that would haunt her for her entire life: Why was the world set up like it was? Why did so many suffer while a few lived a life of happiness and luxury? What was the meaning of life, and why was she put on the earth? And why did so many people seem content to never stop to ask these questions of themselves?

Dorothy finally burst out of the confines of her rather small and sheltered life when she was just sixteen years old, winning a college scholarship with her essays on Greek and Latin. Her father, John Day, was a journalist with strong ideals and stubborn beliefs about the way the world worked. He didn't believe in college education, only allowed his children to read "classic" literature (no radio or newspapers were permitted), and thought the highest aim of a woman was to "stay home and look pretty."[2] But Dorothy's steady diet of literature and her inherited stubbornness made her easily able to defy her father's wishes. She moved to Illinois for college, weeping when she left her toddler brother, John. But beyond the normal pangs of homesickness, Dorothy was thrilled to finally be free to dive headfirst into the realities of the world, away from the limitations of her home.

Tall, angular, and skinny, she was a striking young woman. People told her she had eyes like a doe, set wide on her face and slanting upward. She liked to laugh. She loved learning but didn't feel drawn to her college classes and squandered her scholarship money quickly to purchase books that weren't on the curriculum. When she ran out of money, she ended up getting various odd jobs, and every extra penny went to her beloved friends: the books she devoured and the worlds they opened up. She inhaled Jack London's descriptions of the hard life, Upton Sinclair's idealism, the religious and social imagination of a whole host of Russian authors. She would stay up late into the night, not studying for her classes (which she found boring and not related to the struggles of the poor around her) but instead reading novels that she laundered shirts and watched other people's children in order to buy.

She was thrilled by the hard work and considered it all grist for the mill, a necessary part of her becoming something of a muckraker herself.

Two years after she started, Dorothy dropped out of college, eventually finding her way to New York City. She had found commonality not with her professors but in a small group of radicals—young people who stayed up late dreaming of a better world, one that prioritized the worker. They asked the same question she did: why was the world set up like it was? Dorothy began writing for leftist papers, embarking on experiments in poverty, covering labor issues, writing about strikes, and chronicling the plight of workers demanding basic human rights. She lived in tenement apartments and experienced the hospitality of her poor neighbors firsthand.

She was a natural muckraker, writing detailed descriptions of poverty and the people who endured it while also trying to convince readers to care passionately about the structures that created such misery. One of her first stories in the leftist newspaper *The Call* consisted of Dorothy embarking on an experiment aimed to shame the New York Police Department, which was operating a highly publicized "diet squad" to show how cheaply one could live in New York City. It was an attempt to belittle and put into doubt the stories of extreme poverty and suffering that many people experienced in the city and to ridicule efforts and demands for more aid and relief.

Dorothy, young and full of fire, decided to undergo a "diet squad of one" and wrote about her experiences for the paper. She lived in a tenement on the Lower East Side and wrote about the poverty she experienced there—both the hardships and also the extreme monotony, especially related to the foods one could afford when trying to live on the $1.82 a week that organized charity would have given a single woman like herself.

This was the crash course in life Dorothy had been dreaming of. Sometimes she worked for ten hours a day covering various labor issues and then at night would go out on the town to the

dances and balls put on by the socialists and worker union organizations like the Industrial Workers of the World (IWW). In the
early twentieth century, spirits were high with the thought that
the world could change for the better. The young people knew it
would take a lot of work and struggle but that it could be accomplished together. Picketing, marching, organizing, holding endless
meetings—and then late nights spent dancing, drinking, kissing,
downing coffee, smoking cigarettes, and having conversations that
veered from politics to art to philosophy. And there was Dorothy,
in the midst of it all, electrified by the promise of a better world
made in community.

World War I burst the bubble of idealistic optimism that Dorothy and her newfound friends had built in the blooming bohemian scene of Greenwich Village. The writers and editors Dorothy
palled around with, the majority of whom were men, were either
conscripted into the war or faced long battles to become conscientious objectors. Dorothy, at this point barely in her twenties, was
left in charge as the editor of the socialist paper *The Masses* for
several months until the government officially shut it down—a
remarkable feat for a young, single woman in the early 1900s.[3]
Dorothy was given editorial power and learned the skills necessary to run a magazine while also experiencing the consequences
of publishing radical thought during wartime. When the male
editors of *The Masses* were put on trial, Dorothy was called to
the stand as a witness. According to the court reporter, she was
"belligerent," refusing to talk. The radicals in New York and Chicago, the two cities to which Dorothy was most intimately connected, scattered during those war years. Some went to war, some

went into hiding, and some went to jail. The mood was sour and somber. Fear crept in.

Dorothy got jobs and lost jobs, bouncing around during uncertain times. One of her radical friends Peggy Baird reached out to her during one of her bouts of unemployment and asked Dorothy if she would want to come picket for women's right to vote. Up for an adventure, Dorothy said yes. She went with a group of women to the White House and picketed outside. Up until that day, the women suffragettes had been peaceably broken up every time they protested. But the day Dorothy was there was different. Counter-protestors showed up and brutally attacked the women, including Dorothy (to the point that her fellow protestors were worried for her safety). When the suffragettes were arrested, they were taken to an infamous prison/workhouse in Virginia. There again, Dorothy was assaulted by the police officers in such a violent way it made headlines—her head, neck, and back were nearly broken by the force the officers used on her. She was thrown in a cell with women handcuffed to the bars and then put in solitary confinement, where she and the other prisoners went on a coordinated hunger strike.

Miserable, alone, scared, hungry—these several weeks were horrific for Dorothy. The realities of the treatment of US prisoners made itself known in her body and in her spirit, and she was shaken, searching for comfort. From one of the guards, she ended up requesting a Bible, reading the Psalms on her small cot. Later, she reflected that the words "echoed" in her soul. The feeling of familiarity and comfort she found in the lament and penitent Psalms stayed with her the rest of her days, words targeted to the broken and the despondent—"out of the depths I cry to you, Lord," one psalm read.[4] She was now more acutely aware of who the scriptures were written for—the crushed and broken-hearted—and it ministered to her.

Even in this awful moment of solitary confinement, her muckraking spirit survived. She and her fellow protestors knew they were making headlines, exposing the horrific treatment of prisoners and, with their hunger strike, drawing negative attention that would reach the White House. Was the government okay with the way these women were being treated in prison? Would Woodrow Wilson let these women starve themselves to death? He would not. Eventually, he released them after their ten-day hunger strike, and he later put his support behind the 19th Amendment, which gave white women the right to vote. This was Dorothy's first prison experience, and it would not be her last.

A few years later, while trying to help a friend in crisis, Dorothy was rounded up in a sweep of an IWW flophouse. The police, at this time, regularly conducted raids to round up "radicals" and charged Dorothy and her female friend with prostitution. Again, the experience shook her. She was forced to stand on the street corner while the police interrogated her, while onlookers were led to assume the prostitution accusation. The state of the jail was ghastly, and Dorothy miserably noted how the US justice system seemed to thrive on the dehumanization of the people within the cells. But she also experienced the community of the women inside, their support and care for each other, even in desperate and dire circumstances. All her life, she retained her sense of awe for the people who make up life in the prisons, this hidden world underneath our society, and all that they survived. Every layer of these experiences—writing, protesting, undergoing public humiliation and jail—further connected curiosity to her questions about the world.

While Dorothy did not know it yet, the years of being in the thick of the struggle—for socialism, for the rights of workers, for women's rights (for some women, at least)—and being in relationship to people who were very poor or desolate and had very few options were times of her becoming close to the very people she later understood as those God prioritized over and over again in scriptures. She was trying to live out an ethic she later discovered was articulated by Jesus: "Whatever you have done for the least of these, you have done for me." Later, she recognized Jesus as someone who intimately knew the experiences of the poor when he asked his disciples to clothe the naked, feed the hungry, give water to the thirsty, care for the sick, visit those in prison, and bury the dead. Dorothy did all of those things, and yet when she looked at others also feeding the poor, they were not the Christians. Her comrades were instead leftists, atheists, and socialists. Why would she and her friends ever be interested in a religion that encouraged people to pray in order to forget about the troubles of the world, to feel better about their bourgeois lifestyle?

When she looked at the Christians around her, she saw no common kinship of purpose. Yet, at her most troubled moments, the words of Psalms drifted back to her, comforting her, reminding her of a future and of a past that she couldn't quite remember.

Reminding her of a seemingly impossible dreamed-of world where every prisoner, every person in poverty, every worker exploited to their death was seen and known and loved by God.

This kind of world was too good to be true, she knew. But sometimes, in her darkest moments, she believed it still.

THE LOST GENERATION

You are all a lost generation.

—**Gertrude Stein**, quoted by Ernest Hemingway in
A Sun Also Rises, 1926

Writers, thinkers, and literary types in the early 1920s had lived through an era of incredible upheaval and rapid social change, and they were deconstructing traditional values left and right. This included "values" such as nationalism, strict gender norms, and an upbeat American idealism about a progressively better future. The undoing of these norms produced writers like T. S. Eliot, F. Scott Fitzgerald, Hemingway, and Steinbeck.[1] They were restless wanderers, people with keen eyes for society's inequalities and an appetite for self-destruction. They were people who wrote about the bleak underside of the gilded American dream, and they were all Dorothy Day's contemporaries.

"The Lost Generation" felt they were set apart, different from previous groups, alienated from the cultural norms as never before. They ran headfirst into making the 1920s the "greatest, gaudiest spree in history," as F. Scott Fitzgerald declared it. They all tried to imitate each other, to outdo each other with their novels of drunk young men and women taking on multiple ill-advised lovers, stories full of heartbreak and Hemingway-esque dialogue. They met up in places like Paris and Greenwich Village; they found each other in bars and talked long into the night. They had their own secret songs and words and poems they shared with each other, blissfully sure they were in some sort of cultural and artistic rebellion against "the stuffy people who were misruling the world."[2]

Malcolm Cowley, part of this crowd and eventually the editor of *The New Republic,* characterized this generation in his book *Exile's Return,* published in 1934. In one chapter, Cowley wrote about a bar nicknamed The Hell Hole, a favorite haunt of the Lost Generation—and of Dorothy Day. She would gather there late at night along with the actors and writers. Cowley wrote that the place was full of petty thieves and that "the gangsters admired Dorothy Day because she could drink them under the table; but they felt more at home with Eugene O'Neil, who listened to their troubles and never criticized them."[3]

When Cowley's book was published, Dorothy was apparently furious. To have her years of hobnobbing with the Lost Generation summed up in such a sentence! She took revenge and the narrative back into her own hands when she wrote about this period of her life in *The Long Loneliness.* She never mentioned her proficiency at drinking and carousing and instead focused on how she was trying to connect to others and to God in those heady years. For her, they were times of great searching and chaos—alternately holding people as they died of drug overdoses and listening in rapt attention as a drunk O'Neil would burst forth into a memorized recitation of

"The Hound of Heaven," a religious poem published in 1893 about not being able to escape the divine love of God. Some of her bohemian friends told her she had always been haunted—pursued—by God, and she felt this in her bones. No matter how hard she tried to outrun God, she could never run fast or far enough. But for a few years, she truly did try.

The description of the Lost Generation encapsulates this period of Dorothy's life. The wandering and disillusionment, breaking free from old traditions but not being quite sure what to replace them with. This affected both her professional literary career and her personal life. The idealism at the turn of the twentieth century was quieted by death and destruction on a massive scale—unions could no longer save the world when it was going to hell in World War I. And then came the deadly flu, wiping out the last traces of optimism many of these idealists clung to. Commonly known as the Spanish flu, or the influenza of 1918, it swept through New York City at the tail end of World War I. Before COVID-19, it was the deadliest pandemic the United States had seen, and cities like New York were greatly impacted.

When the Spanish flu hit, Dorothy was twenty years old. Sensing the dire needs of the time, she decided to become a nurse, training and working at a public hospital for the poor. It was a blur of hard work and camaraderie, her own personal war effort aimed at overcoming the spread of illness. Dorothy learned how to survive in extreme situations and particularly appreciated how the Catholic sisters who ran the hospital organized the day around prayer and stopping for meals amid the never-ending and often crushing work. This dedication to daily renewal impressed itself upon Dorothy as a way to survive what might seem unimaginable: stopping for prayer, a hot cup of coffee, a good sandwich—and one can get back to work.

Considering the span and trajectory of Dorothy Day's life, it is not a surprise that in many ways, she enjoyed being in the thick of the struggle to beat the influenza of 1918. She worked in hospitals that were a last stop for the poor, and she took care of people who were dying alone. In her later recollections, she never mentioned a fear of death for herself—even as the flu tended to target and kill young, healthy men and some women her age. Instead, it was days and days of being at the frontline of help and finding solace in the routine and comfort of her co-laborers. Even before she had the language for it, she enjoyed being the hands and feet of Jesus in caring for others.

But after a year of nursing under extreme circumstances, Dorothy Day did something she had never done before. She fell head-over-heels in love with a man. His name was Lionel Moise, a vibrant, hard-drinking Jewish newspaperman, the kind of man who could get a good story out of anyone.[4] He was Dorothy's first real love, and her relationship with him was fast, intense, and ended with unimaginable heartbreak. But Dorothy rarely wrote about this time in her life, nor did it neatly fit into the thread lines she liked to point out in her memoirs: her longing for God or her desire for social change. Her granddaughter, Kate Hennessy, would later write about this time in Dorothy's life in her exquisitely rendered memoir/biography.[5] Hennessy mused that perhaps it was

Moise's vigor and zest for life (coupled with his being a writer and creative) that made a tired and worn-out nurse fall quite so hard for Lionel. It's hard to say, for this experience was out of character for Dorothy. And she had little to say to the world about her personal heartbreaks—except for the one time she did.

In 1924, Dorothy published a semiautobiographical novel called *The Eleventh Virgin*. It focuses on a period in her life that she glossed over constantly in her own nonfiction writings (in *The Long Loneliness*, shortly after describing her work in the hospital, she says, "In trying to write about the next few years of my life I find there is little to say"[6]). It's a novel about a nurse who falls in love with a patient, moves in with him, enters into an unhealthy obsessive relationship, becomes pregnant, and then has an abortion as a last-ditch effort to keep her lover (who abandons her anyway). *The New York Times* panned it when it first came out, saying it was like every other adolescent novel ever written. Her literary friends, who were supportive at first, ultimately agreed with the critics. It was not a well-written book. It soon faded from the public consciousness but never from Dorothy's mind. Later in her life, she declared it was such a bad novel that she wished she could buy every copy out of existence. She used to dream of finding copies of it in used bookstores and destroying them all, burning them in a fire.

Conscious that I was embarking on a betrayal of sorts, I read *The Eleventh Virgin*. The novel revolves around a woman's infatuation with a man who is neither kind nor good. Reading it, the style and approach feel dated, but what stood out to me about *The Eleventh Virgin* was how little it resembled everything else I had read by Dorothy. The dialogue was flat, the pacing was terrible, and it was as though she was imitating the cool and removed dramatic novels of her time.

What most readers focus on is the book's ending, when June (the main character) has a backdoor abortion. It reminded me of the complexities of talking about abortion in the context of toxic relationships and societies that make it almost impossible for a young, poor, single woman to be a mother. Without pity, the novel expresses the complexity, sadness, and trauma of her situation. The doctor who provides the abortion for June is a woman—a widow who takes in illegal clients like June to support her own son and provide a house, food, and schooling for him. It describes the bodily suffering and the humiliation June experiences when her lover refuses to pick her up after the abortion, instead leaving her with a note on her pincushion saying they are through. This is how the book ends, with June being all alone.

Dorothy Day was someone—for all her bluster, hard-drinking socialist comrades, prison stays, and more—who experienced pain and complex relationships just like any other woman. She was someone who had to grow up very fast and support herself in a patriarchal, capitalistic society with little to no social safety nets. *The Eleventh Virgin* reveals Dorothy to be a real person instead of a cardboard cutout saint. It also reveals a narrative slightly more complex than what I understood on my first reading of the text. While Dorothy was traumatized by her relationship with Lionel and suffered immense heartbreak, *The Eleventh Virgin* is not a cautionary tale warning young women away from abortions. In many ways, it was the story of a liberated woman in love and one who would have wished for safer and legal conditions to end her pregnancy. In 1924, Dorothy Day was an admirer of Margaret Sanger (her sister Della worked with Sanger for a time). Longtime Catholic Worker and friend of Dorothy's Brian Terrell notes that if it was an antiabortion book, Dorothy would most likely have incorporated that into her autobiographies and Catholic testimony. Instead, she wanted to erase its existence.

The Eleventh Virgin is a true story, Dorothy admitted, but it is also highly fictionalized. Biographers have pointed out that Dorothy's own abortion—and the aftermath she endured—was much worse than the stylized account she gave in her novel.[7] But no matter how people would like to weaponize Dorothy's past— both her abortion and the novel she wrote about it—Dorothy herself mostly refused to enter into the political conversation about abortion rights after her conversion to Catholicism. Indeed, her paper covered all manner of controversial topics, but as early as 1935, she said that it would not be touching on the issue of birth control at all. Her public comments on abortion in her long and storied life are few and far between, but the common link is a deep well of understanding the pain and individual circumstances surrounding abortions. Terrell further pointed out that Dorothy never spoke, wrote, or marched in favor of criminalizing abortion and that "laws against abortion offered her no protection but only added more pain, destruction and degradation to a most wretched experience in her life."[8] Her pain quieted her. And this should mean something to us all.

In real life, Dorothy struggled to move on from both Lionel and her abortion. In fact, she moved across the country to follow him (and even helped to console other desperate women who had been jilted by him). In this time period, she tried to die by suicide twice, before friends intervened. In an abrupt attempt to change course, she married a wealthy, hard-partying man named Berkley Tobey, many years her senior, and sailed off to Europe with him.[9] "I married him on the rebound," she said simply, later on. Dorothy tried for a minute to take on the role of a wife and wealthy novel-writing expatriate (working on the manuscript that would eventually turn into *The Eleventh Virgin*), but it didn't stick. She just as quickly divorced her new husband and then returned to Chicago to try to convince Moise to come back to her. She then fled him and moved to New Orleans and then New York City, trying to focus on her writing again. Eventually, *The Eleventh Virgin* was accepted and published by the Boni Brothers. Dorothy worked on a second novel, and she continued to spend much of her time in the city with the literary crowd. These were restless, circular years but also years of growth as she regained independence, confidence, and her liberated ways.

Dorothy admitted that, for a time, she was lost in the world, but even in those years, she was always watchful, always listening, wide open to the world, to all the ways it could be made better or different—and always with a knack for finding herself smack dab in the middle of all the action. Later in life, as Dorothy lived at the New York City Catholic Worker house during the turbulent '60s and '70s, the times of free love and peace and music and drugs, she wrote about how she identified with the new generation of the time. Perhaps she thought of them as the next iteration of the Lost Generation. She herself had lived out the very same experience— save for the drugs—decades earlier. It was a part of being in the thick of things, of chasing the liberated path in a time of cultural shifts.

But she was aware the toll had been high for her as a young woman in the 1920s, and despite finding some grounding after Europe, Chicago, New Orleans, and the return to New York, she was starting to feel worn, tired. While she continued to love writing, the disaster of World War I and the scattering of her radical friends had her evaluating her optimism for the future. The Roaring Twenties had not been kind to her thus far, with multiple heartbreaks and a long string of odd jobs as she struggled to pay her bills. The time of expatriate travels and her rebound relationship in Europe left Dorothy a bit unmoored. At twenty-seven, she felt older than her years; she had seen her share of the world and its problems and didn't know what the solutions were anymore. She had experienced love and lost it. She had published a novel and found it didn't bring her success or happiness. Where was she to go next?

I think about young Dorothy, eating apples in her chair at her childhood Chicago home, dreaming about the world. I think about her tromping around New York City and showing up to boring union meetings and reporting on picketing lines, her bright face and girlish laugh punctuating her intense ideals. I think about her nursing the poor and the sick, up to her elbows in chaos and despair in an influenza pandemic. I think about her having her heart absolutely trampled in the tender experience of being a woman in love with someone who did not love her in the ways she needed. And I also think about her fretting later in life about the novel she wrote exposing her very soul and vulnerability as a young woman—wishing she could go into every bookstore in the world and buy up every last copy and burn it so it would be as if the novel never existed.[10]

She was a lost soul in a lost generation, yet it made her who she was. One of Dorothy's favorite Dostoevsky quotes declares that "compassion is the chief law of human existence," and it is compassion I feel when it comes to looking at this period in Dorothy's life. Compassion both for her situation and for all the young women caught in her exact same and terrible circumstances. And also compassion for older Dorothy, who tossed and turned at night, dreaming about destroying the work that set her story frozen in time, where anyone could read and judge it. Her experience made her tender to the pain of other women for the rest of her life; I hope she put some of that tenderness toward herself too. I hope at some point that she would have seen herself as a perfect, flawed human—someone made in the image of the invisible God. That's what I feel when I read her novel and when I read her own descriptions of her life. She is a beautiful, complicated person. Just like all of us.

A CONVERSION OF JOY

I always loved you more than you did me.

—Dorothy Day to Forster Batterham, December 1932,
All the Way to Heaven

While people who only know Dorothy through her writings or pictures tended to think of her as sharp and grim, a common refrain from those who knew her was that she was a beautiful woman. Striking, luminous, unforgettable. Her combination of handsomeness, gregariousness, intellect, and quick wit attracted people to her throughout her entire life.

Forster Batterham was no exception. The brother of one of Dorothy's radical friends—socialists, bohemian types—he was among the number who loved to drink and gather and talk through ideas of a better world.

Tall, quiet, and reserved, he was the opposite of Dorothy in many ways. In a rush, they fell in love, a love that gave birth in many ways to the next chapter of her life. When Dorothy Day wrote her foundational work, *The Long Loneliness*, she titled part two of the book "Natural Happiness" and began the section with these words: "The man I loved, with whom I entered into a common-law marriage, was an anarchist, an Englishman by descent, and a biologist."[1]

The film rights had been sold to *The Eleventh Virgin*, and with that money, Dorothy Day bought a small beach shack on Staten Island. Forster moved in almost right away, where together they blended into a small community of bohemians looking to escape the city. He commuted into New York City for his job during the week making gauges at a factory, as Dorothy stayed home, writing freelance articles for radical newspapers, puttering around and cooking over a fire, and walking miles along the shore each day. She holed up during stormy weather, reading Russian novels, Dickens, the Bible, and *The Imitation of Christ* by the fire. In the winter evenings, Forster, a naturalist, studied star charts, and together they would walk on the beach and look up into the night sky. Dorothy was overwhelmed and entranced by all there was to learn, if only one knew where and how to look.

As I read of Dorothy's life in those months in *The Long Loneliness*, I could almost smell the salt and smoke of the cold beach living they sank into and noticed, between the words, her building resilience and healing from war, illness, and personal trauma, one book and one constellation at a time.

This is how Dorothy herself frames this period in her life, settling on a few phrases—*utter happiness, domesticity, simple living away from the city, long walks with Forster*—contributing to her peaceful joy. As she later reflected on her conversion to Catholicism, she tried to insist that it wasn't unhappiness with the world that caused the turn but that it was only when she was finally and truly happy—in love, living on the beach, pregnant—that she turned to God.

During that time in her beach shack on Staten Island, Dorothy found herself praying as she cleaned and cooked. As she took the train into the New York City, she'd clutch a rosary given to her by a friend. Soon, she started attending Mass on Sundays at a nearby church.

While she headed to Sunday-morning Mass, she would struggle with herself, wondering why she was doing any of this. *Remember what Marx said,* she would tell herself—*that religion was the opiate of the masses?* As her fingers touched the beads on the rosary in her pocket, she'd tell herself, "You are in a stupor of contentment—you are biological, like a cow."[2] Was she turning into a placid, unquestioning, rote religious person? Almost as soon as she would question herself, she immediately argued back with herself, reasoning this wasn't medicating or numbing herself with religion; all she was doing was thanking God. She wasn't asking or pleading for anything. She was simply expressing gratitude for her life and the joy she now found in it.

But that very drive toward the Divine, Dorothy knew, would eventually pull her from the place of contentment she currently inhabited: "It was a peace, curiously enough, divided against itself. I was happy but my very happiness made me know that there was a greater happiness to be obtained from life than any I had ever known."[3]

When Dorothy got pregnant, it filled her cup almost to overflowing with joy. And as hard as it is to understand, the more she experienced this natural happiness, the clearer she saw her path forward being divided into two. She knew Forster and his ideological beliefs would eventually force her to a choice about what she ultimately wanted in her engagement with the world in all its beauty, yes, but also its suffering.

And so Dorothy, at twenty-nine, pregnant, happy, rosary beads in tow, decided to upend her life once again.

Forster and the Catholic Church were at odds with each other. He rebelled against the institution of the family, declaring himself an anarchist against "the tyranny of love." He hated both religion and institutional authority and couldn't comprehend how Dorothy was drawn to the Catholic Church—the worst of both, to his thinking. Their arguments grew louder and more fraught. Dorothy, always drawn to idealists, at first found Forster's stubbornness inspiring—and then exasperating. He refused to entertain the idea of marriage and didn't want to bring children into this sordid world. He did not grow up poor, and yet the subject of income inequality gnawed at him constantly. He had never been imprisoned, yet he read loudly, passionately from the newspaper every morning to Dorothy of those who had. What he did with his anguish at the state of the world, she wrote years later, was to further retreat from it, to build a smaller world from the shell of his garden and fishing boat, to sail away from all that troubled him.

Perhaps for a time, Dorothy thought she could make it work with such a person. And then she experienced a miracle. Having lived for years with the burden that her abortion may have left her sterile, one hot summer day, at a party with some of their friends, eating pickled eels and popcorn and drinking root beer, she suddenly realized she was pregnant with Forster's child. She remembered the smells, the tastes, and her "blissful joy." Becoming pregnant brought her delight and also solidified her path forward in life. This was her tangible proof, her sign of a loving God. A gift she did not dare to believe could be hers.

Forster did not believe in miracles, nor was he initially pleased that Dorothy was pregnant (though, as Dorothy hoped, he eventually fell in love with the child). Dorothy didn't care. She happily got to work preparing her house. And in the last few months of her pregnancy, she moved to the city to be closer to medical care, living with her sister Della. As her belly grew, so did her religious leanings and her mysterious joy in the miracle of conception. Dorothy reread books like *The Imitation of Christ*, thinking about how she wanted to raise her child. Some of her bohemian friends seemed at a loss when it came to talking to their children about morals or ethics, which she felt found a natural language in religion. She wanted her child to grow up with a strong religious framework, to grow up as part of something that she herself always wished she had been born into.

In the cold apartment in New York, she made her decision: once she had her baby, that child would be baptized in the Catholic Church. And she knew that, soon enough, she would convert as well. She tried to feel happy about this decision but couldn't fully celebrate because she knew that baptizing her child and converting to organized religion would also involve a death of sorts. The death of her few years of natural happiness, the joy of a kind man in her bed, of a life spent filled with a home bursting with children and laughter and ideals. In her books, she writes it was all a conversion of joy, but I see something different. I see sorrow written into nearly every line of her conversion story. And I think she saw it too.

Dorothy did baptize her baby in a local Catholic Church. Forster didn't attend the ceremony but caught fresh lobster to feed everyone at a party held at their shack afterward. Dorothy was ebullient, celebrating this momentous occasion with friends and family, which made Forster furious. He abruptly left the party, not to reappear for several days. The anger and the absences soon became a commonplace occurrence for them—with fights about Dorothy's pull toward religion and his inability to commit. Storming off for days, he would return, sheepish. And Dorothy always let him back in.

She dreamed of marrying Forster and having a house full to bursting with children, but he refused to get married in front of either church or state. Now that her child was Catholic, Dorothy would soon follow. And here was the crux of the problem: the Catholic Church would not allow her in since she was living in sin with Forster. She begged Forster to marry, to soften his ideals and anarchism just this once. She promised not to hang up pictures of Jesus all over the walls. *You won't even notice. Just let me be me, in all of my religious fervor*, she said.

But he could not—or would not.

Despite insisting her conversion centered around joy, scattered clues indicate this was a terrible time for Dorothy internally. She became overwhelmed, so oppressed by the considerations for her future that she could not even breathe, panicking, struggling for air. She went to the doctor. Was it her thyroid? No, the doctor said. She was suffering from a nervous condition, the result of her inner turmoil.

Her body was trying to tell her what her heart longed to ignore. Then one night, Dorothy and Forster had another fight about religion. He left in one of his protests to sleep on the beach. When he came back to the house, Dorothy barred the door with her body. No more, she said. This agonizing back and forth had to stop, and she would need to be the one to do it.

The next day, she left her shack determined; a year and a half after baptizing her daughter into the Catholic Church, Dorothy herself entered under a conditional baptism. She left her baby with a friend and went by herself to the church, grimly determined to take the next steps forward in faith. She went into the church alone and came out alone, a fact I think about often.

Later, a priest urged her to write about her conversion experience and how it was the social teachings of the Church that drew her to it. She protested, saying she had never heard the social teachings and had never read an encyclical. In *The Long Loneliness*, she makes the struggle plain:

> I felt that the church was the church of the poor . . . that it cared for the emigrant, it established hospitals, orphanages, day nurseries, houses of the Good Shepherd, homes of the aged, but at the same time, I felt it did not set its face

against a social order which made so much charity in the present sense of the word necessary. I felt that charity was a word to choke over. Who wanted charity? And it was not just man's pride but a strong sense of man's dignity and worth, and what was due to him in justice, that made me resent, rather than feel proud of so mighty a sum total of Catholic institutions.[4]

She still primarily thought of the Church as an organization that was often at odds with justice, but in its core doctrines concerning the dignity of life, she saw a theology she could work with—a tension many people live with to this day.

One of the things I love best about Dorothy Day is that she never did anything halfway. She had been told that the Catholic Church was the church of the poor and the historic true church, so that is where she would pledge herself. And she knew the second she did, she would lose what little stability she had created for herself on that windswept beach on Staten Island. How I wish there had been more people to celebrate her joy with her; how I wish she had been baptized while surrounded by friends and coconspirators and loved ones—Forster and her siblings and her bohemian friends and neighbors. But few among her beloved circle understood this aspect of Dorothy, even as they knew she was haunted by God. As she made her yearnings public, she was alone in her conviction that she was doing what was right.

On her own, she turned toward the place her joy kept pulling. She turned toward a Love that would never abandon her, even as it made her life lonelier.

THE MIRACLE OF LOVE

I had heard many say that they wanted to worship
God in their own way and did not need a Church in
which to praise Him . . . but I did not agree to this.
My very experience as a radical, my whole make-up,
led me to want to associate myself with others, with
the masses, in loving and praising God.

—**Dorothy Day**, *The Long Loneliness*

Dorothy's conversion story is intricately connected to the miracle love of her life—her daughter, Tamar—and how her conception, birth, and life were born of both sadness and joy. Mothers around the world understand this complexity: bringing life into the world clarifies the mind, sharpens the eyes to see both miracles and terrors. It's a space where the veil between life and death is thin, and Dorothy's religious leanings took on a new fervor when she became what she called a "co-laborer" with God in giving birth to a child.

I, too, have felt the thin spaces surrounding childbirth and motherhood, how they connect us to God and to each other. And how they also invite us into spaces of potential grief. At age twenty-six, I almost died due to complications from my first pregnancy. My child was born several months early, and for a week I couldn't hold my tiny baby; when I finally could, both of us were connected to so many wires and machines, it was a beeping, tangled mess. My life changed abruptly. The birth of my child was the end of so many things for me: my innocence, my sense of immortality, my nonstop rushing in a capitalistic society, benefiting from a society I never questioned.

Now here was my baby: tiny, immune-compromised. For the first year of her life, I stayed home and took care of her. The life of working multiple part-time jobs, finishing up a master's degree in education, and being involved in numerous English classes and afterschool programs for refugee and immigrant friends and neighbors at our apartment complex came to a halt. In the year of change, I rocked and rocked my sad baby, alarmed by the harsh and bright and noisy world she had been born into.

Within this space, stillness, solitude, and grief, something unfurled within me. It allowed me to process a life of pelting pell-mell toward making money, acquiring education, and doing good works for the Lord. When my baby napped, I would start to type out a few words on my computer. When words began to tell me things about myself I had been too scared to say or even think aloud, I met myself in astonishment.

I think about this time in my own life when I turn to the story of Dorothy and the miracle of her daughter, Tamar—the tangled emotions and existence integral to Dorothy's work. Having a baby changed everything for her. For Dorothy, the birth of Tamar was an explosion of life and joy and love toward God, perhaps the most important moment of conversion in her entire life.

Dorothy named her baby Tamar Teresa. *Teresa* after St. Teresa of Avila, whose writings influenced her, and *Tamar* because she had heard the name shouted out at various children in her neighborhood and thought it sounded beautiful. *Tamar*, she knew, meant "palm tree" and was a biblical name. Dorothy later read the Hebrew scriptures and discovered that the two women named Tamar therein suffered brutal violence in the stories of the patriarchs, and she was dismayed. She didn't know this history when she named her baby. As a gift from God, she wanted a beautiful, religious name for her daughter that honored the miracle.

A name filled with beauty and sadness and religion is a fitting start for Tamar Teresa. As an infant, she was baptized into the Catholic Church, starting the chain of events that would cause Dorothy to convert the next year. Tamar, often a silent and wide-eyed spectator in the story of Dorothy Day's life, later provided a lens for many to understand aspects of Dorothy's personality that often get overlooked by her biographers, the majority of whom are male. Dorothy and Tamar had a complicated relationship articulated best in the book *Beauty Will Save the World*, written by Tamar's youngest daughter, Kate Hennessy. Through years of talks and interviews and conversations peppered with long silences, Kate began to draw out the voice of her mother, Tamar, when it came to Dorothy.

It is through Tamar we learned of Dorothy's enduring love for Forster, how the loss of him stayed with her throughout her life.

Tamar kept the letters Forster had saved from Dorothy. For years after they separated, Dorothy wrote to Forster, struggling with her love and desire for him: "*I dream of you every night—that I am lying in your arms and I can feel your kisses and it tortures me, but so sweet too. I do love you more than anything else in the world, but I cannot help my religious sense, which tortures me unless I do as I believe is right.*" She wrote angry missives too: "*Do I have to be condemned to celibacy all my days because of your pigheadedness?*" And as she struggled with their child's care and financial challenges, she also wrote in frustration: "*I wonder how you would feel if one of your sisters had to go through the struggle I do . . . and that the man was indeed a most pig-headed idiot to ruin their two lives.*"

Dorothy, desperate to flee the temptation of going back to her tumultuous relationship with Forster, moved constantly throughout Tamar's childhood. As a result, Tamar did not spend much time with her father. Tamar later in life said, "I guess we'd been very close when I was an infant, but of course I don't really remember that. I think I missed [my father] terribly, you know, in an unconscious way."

For some time, Tamar and Dorothy continued living in Staten Island. Dorothy drove a set of ramshackle cars around the beaches, interviewing residents about their gardens for freelance articles. Then they moved to California, where Dorothy tried her hand in Hollywood to make a bit of money. The dream only lasted a few months before the Great Depression hit and she was laid off by the movie studio. In many ways, she was relieved—she was stifled and bored sitting in an office reading novels that might be optioned into movie scripts.

She would, she decided, drive a car down to Mexico and live there with Tamar for as long as her money would last.[1] They lived in a small apartment, and Dorothy soaked in the warmth and atmosphere. She dragged Tamar to Mass, thrilled at being surrounded by devout Mexican Catholics.

After Tamar contracted malaria, they left to visit Dorothy's mother in Florida, where Tamar could receive medical care. Dorothy stayed in Florida but traveled for articles and took Tamar along. In her *House of Hospitality,* Dorothy writes that those five years of Tamar's early life were cobbled together with odd jobs: bookseller, cook, research worker, synopsis and dialogue writer, and newspaper correspondent. The stories from this time revealed, among other things, Tamar as a bright, inquisitive child; her love for her mother; and her desire to imitate Dorothy's religious leanings.

In one of her first-ever pieces for the Catholic magazine *Commonweal,* Dorothy wrote a rambling, lively story of taking four-year-old Tamar to visit Our Mother of Guadalupe in Mexico City.[2] "A pil'mage?" Tamar asks her mother hopefully, stripping Dorothy's hard-earned marigold blossoms from the stems around their apartment to spill at the feet of Mary, who lived in a chapel. Dorothy described the crowded bus ride, Tamar's made-up songs about the animals who shared seats with their neighbors, and the good humor of those on the bus. Distracted by all the animals crowding the streets and stalls and the people selling rosaries, candles, and sweets near the shrine, Tamar declares, "These are all Mary's babies. . . . The little pigs and the chickens and the boys and the girls. And these are all little baby houses, and that," she said, pointing to the church, "is the mama house."

Mixed into Dorothy's delight at her little theologian are also commentaries about the conditions of the working poor in Mexico City and the hardscrabble lives of poverty—especially those of the women. Mother Mary is venerated, adored, and present in the lives of people in need of shelter from a harsh and cruel world. This and other writings focus on this triangle of the world: her delight in Tamar; Mary, the mother of God; and the harsh and dreadful and beautiful world that they all existed in together. Dorothy was drawn to all of it. As a single mother, she looked constantly to Mother Mary. She was pulled to a religion that consecrated the beauty of nurturing life, even in the hardest of times.

I love gleaning any information I can about Tamar. She is often ignored or pushed aside in the stories written about her mother. But especially in the beginning, her mother couldn't stop writing *about her*. As she got older, Tamar stubbornly refused to baptize the image of her mother that was popularized as a strict and determined saint. When she was a young girl, Tamar viewed Dorothy as the sun around which she got her sustenance: her joyful, energetic, funny mother. Tamar hated how her mother tended to look grim and severe in published photographs, a no-nonsense religious activist, because they didn't capture the totality of who Dorothy was. She was the light in Tamar's life, all-absorbing and all-encompassing.

The feeling was mutual. A beautiful picture into this time of Dorothy's emotional life was the piece she wrote from her hospital bed in the days after giving birth to Tamar. Her joy, awe, and gratitude explode with exuberance from the page. That piece, called "Having a Baby," was published in *The New Masses*, where it became extremely popular with socialists and communists the world over, endearing Dorothy to comrades in Latin America and Soviet Russia. The entire piece combines Dorothy's cheekiness and powers of observation with her deep wells of love as it moves from Dorothy's labor pains through to her marveling at the miracle of tiny Tamar Teresa and the human need to survive and to love.

This piece also reveals the often unexplored Dorothy Day: her funny descriptions of the experience of giving birth (she and her friend Carol frantically sharing a cigarette in the taxi on the way to the hospital, for instance) as well as her subversive insights. At one point, in the throes of contractions, Dorothy thinks about childbirth as a universal experience reflected in the novels she loved so much and read that winter: novels by Upton Sinclair, Leo Tolstoy, and Eugene O'Neil. Realizing these novels were all written by men, she turns suddenly angry in a burst of labor pains and frustration: "*What did these men know about it? It was so much funnier, painful, and absurd than they had made it out to be!*" She comforted herself in the endless hours of labor, imagining how these male writers would respond to the pains of childbirth themselves. And then, just to spite them, she wrote in detail of her own experience of labor just four days after giving birth, to set the record straight.

"Having a Baby"[3] explores the universality of how bringing life into the world connects us to something bigger than ourselves.[4] With Dorothy's journalistic eye for detail plus her lived experience, she was able to reveal the misogyny of the literary world that rarely allowed women to write about their own experiences.

Funny, profound, irreverent, grateful—she was a writer to reckon with.

As she continued her transition to becoming Catholic, she wrote freelance articles for publications like *Commonweal* and *America*, mostly about the joys of mothering. For these few years, there is little about the larger state of the world that Dorothy later focuses on. Instead there was a smallness, a stillness, a keen observance of the world that she sees around her, the seeds of which would continue to make her writing about the everyday life of the Catholic Worker so engaging to her readers.

In Dorothy's own telling, the birth of her daughter changed everything. She joined the masses of humanity who had given birth, who had been awed by cocreation. The sadness of the past few years and decades—the wrenching last chapter of her novel *The Eleventh Virgin*, her break with Forster—all of that is changed by the miraculous arrival of Tamar Teresa. From California to Mexico City to Florida, Dorothy and Tamar watched the devout women who made up the backbone of the Church. Together, they were formed by communities of suffering, religious devotion, and resilience. And Dorothy began to carry these stories of suffering with her—as well as an image of Mother Mary—even if there wasn't a shrine in sight.

THE MIRACLE OF MARY

My soul glorifies the Lord,
my spirit rejoices in God my Savior
for he has been mindful of the humble state of his servant.
From now on all generations will call me blessed:
For the Mighty One has done great things for me,
Holy is his Name.
His mercy extends to those who fear him
From generation to generation.
He has performed mighty deeds with the strength of his arm,
He has scattered those who are proud in their inmost thoughts.
He has brought down the rulers from their thrones,
But has lifted up the humble.
He has filled the hungry with good things,
But has sent the rich away empty.

—**Mary's Magnificat,** the Gospel of Luke

After the years of wandering, floating along to job after job, visiting churches and praying the rosary, Dorothy and Tamar returned to New York City in the thick of the Great Depression. At first, Dorothy moved them to the West Side to be near her beloved Mother of Guadalupe Catholic Church to attend Mass daily. But while living there, Dorothy became sick with a terrible intestinal influenza. The years of trying to provide for herself and her child, of constantly moving, of being a wanderer, strong and solo, were catching up with her. She lay in bed, while Tamar mostly fended for herself. Dorothy was terrified of dying, leaving Tamar without support—how long would it take people to find her daughter?

As she stayed in bed, sick and desperate, she ached for the community and neighborliness of the East Village. On the West Side, she was surrounded by "the ordinary American with his own desire for privacy, for going his own way." The American dream of prosperity and individuality left her lonely and vulnerable. She resolved that when she recovered, she would move back to the East Side, where neighbors—most of them recently arrived immigrants, many of them Catholic and Jewish—took care of each other. It was a plan she stayed true to the rest of her life, and she continued in her awe of the hospitality of people in poverty and of those from more collectivist cultures.

It's hard to imagine the houses of hospitality for the poor springing up in middle-class neighborhoods—a lesson Dorothy learned suffering alone in her apartment with a three-year-old. The terror of that time never left her, and she never wanted another person to experience the kind of loneliness, suffering, and fear that she did.

Dorothy rented out her Staten Island beach house for six months, allowing her and Tamar to afford a tenement apartment in the city for twenty-eight dollars a month. The tenement build-ings were a particular hallmark of the Lower East Side, and Dor-othy lived among the urban poor.[1] Eventually, Dorothy's brother John and his new wife, Tessa, moved in with her and Tamar, mak-ing the four-hundred-square-foot space officially cozy. The apart-ment wasn't much—no hot water and smelly communal toilets in the hallways shared with other families—but it was a home where they were all together.

Once again, Dorothy could not escape the constant reality of poverty. She observed how the Great Depression affected the lives of so many people in her neighborhood. Every day, she saw the men who came from all around the country lining up for work, for bread, for soup, for a place to sleep. She was surrounded on all sides by immigrant families, many of whom had suffered greatly to come to America only to be packed into tiny apartments with few utilities or spots of restorative beauty, green spaces. Once again, Dorothy put back on her intrepid journalist hat, paying careful attention to the people she saw every day and the economic con-ditions that affected them. Once again, Dorothy started to write about labor and economic and racial issues, and now she aimed her insights at the heart of a religious audience.

"I was very upset by what I saw—the church's apparent indif-ference to so much suffering," she wrote. The Great Depression had made such suffering and such intense disparity highly visi-ble, especially in New York City. To her it was inescapable. She saw people wandering the streets, hundreds of them, begging for money and food and work. Everywhere she looked, God's children were abused by systems that overlooked them. And she decided she wasn't going to let it happen without asking the whole world to do something about it. Starting with the church.

Dorothy brought her unique background of leftist muckraking journalism to the Catholic publications that started to hire her. Her years of reporting on labor issues coincided with growing national interest in union workers marching and striking for basic human rights in 1932. The headlines were filled with stories of these men and the terrible conditions they were protesting—including farmers being evicted from their own land after working it for decades and union tradesmen unable to find work and given no relief to even feed their families. Growing around her was an interest in understanding the importance of a united and organized resistance movement as the rich continued to get richer while the average person had less and less to rely on. It was a desperate time for many people. Before the New Deal was implemented starting in 1933, the United States had very few social safety nets—and Dorothy knew that what little existed had been earned by the blood, sweat, and tears of the same people who continued to fight for the rights of their fellow worker.

Dorothy Day was thirty-five when she took an assignment from *Commonweal*[2] to cover a hunger march from New York to Washington, DC, organized by unemployed union workers at the end of 1932. The group was communist-led, although Dorothy observed that the vast majority involved in the march were not communists but people who saw the communists as helping them secure rights for themselves by organizing effectively.[3] "The demands of the marchers were for social legislation, for unemployment insurance, for old-age pensions, for relief for mothers and children, for work," she wrote. The march was planned as a visual tactic meant to stir up emotions—"the communists love drama," Dorothy wrote drily. These men and women marching through small towns and eventually appearing before Congress hoped they would touch the hearts of the average American.

For weeks, the local communist tabloid paper the *Daily Worker* had been publishing plans for the march. Dorothy was on assignment in Union Square where all the protestors gathered to begin the march. The mood was joyful and jubilant, she recollected, as the marchers poured into the city.

But the journey to Washington was fraught for the marchers. At one point, three thousand of them were trapped in a half-mile stretch of roadway, surrounded on all sides by armed forces and citizens' militias determined to stop the "radicals" from storming Washington. Violence broke out against the marchers. The nation's capital was in full panic. Dorothy blamed the newspapers and journalists who consistently painted these men and women as dangerous radicals aiming to overthrow the government. But eventually, the hunger marchers delivered their petition of demands to Congress and then dispersed back to their various cities, hoping for real change.

Scribbling away in her notebook as she watched these tired and beaten and harassed men and women make their way to the place of power and prominence in her country, Dorothy was starting to have a crisis of the heart. She later wrote in *The Long Loneliness* about the moment when the three thousand marchers finally got to Washington, DC: "I stood on the curb and watched them, joy and pride in the courage of this band of men and women moaning in my heart, and with it a bitterness too that since I was now a Catholic, with fundamental philosophical differences, I could not be out there with them. I could write, I could protest to arouse the conscious, but where was the Catholic leadership in the gathering bands of men and women together, for the actual works of mercy?"

For Dorothy, nearly five years a Catholic, it was important to distinguish herself from communists—for personal and philosophical reasons but also so that the Catholic readers she hoped to educate would trust her. The communists had made it clear time and time again that religion was an enemy of their cause, an opiate of the masses, a stumbling block to real social change. The Catholic Church, they said, was in many ways enemy number one, its patriarchal, hierarchical, institutional ideologies at odds with the egalitarian, socialist, and communitarian values they held.

Dorothy chafed at these communists who demanded people walk away from religion to join the class struggle. She was angry at how they overlooked the reality that large percentages of the poor workers around the world were not only religious but Catholic. How could one claim to be for the common worker of the world and dismiss their religion as intellectually depraved and morally corrupt?

All of these thoughts swirled around her at this moment. Here she was, writing about this incredible moment in US history—the economic effects of the Great Depression, the struggle of the worker to organize and demand rights, the tensions between right and left, the violence of police, and the pull of the newspapers to sell more copies—and she was writing about it all for a Catholic magazine. She ached to throw down her pen and join in the march. But she felt as if she couldn't, trapped by her desire to be a good Catholic.

But what good was being a "good" Catholic anyway? "How little, how puny my work had been since becoming a Catholic, I thought," wrote Dorothy. "How self-centered, how ingrown, how lacking in a sense of community! My summer of quiet reading and prayer, my self-absorption seemed single as I watched my brothers in their struggle, not for themselves but for others."[4] As she questioned her own path toward religious holiness, she had an almost-mystical experience watching these bedraggled, hungry, thirsty men and women walk those last few miles to the Capitol building. She watched them, skilled and unskilled, unionized and not, workers who were poor and suffering and driven by desperation and hope for better things—she saw them and, with a sudden realization, concluded that if Jesus were alive today, this is where he would be.

Jesus, the Christ, was an unskilled, low-wage worker. So were all of his friends. Not only would he be a part of the hunger march, Dorothy thought, but if she squinted her eyes just right, she could actually see the face of Christ in the people straggling past her. But this is not what she wrote in her reportage. Not yet, anyway. For now, she had no one to tell about her divine revelations, so she kept them to herself.

In Washington, DC, Dorothy was left to struggle to make sense of what she saw and experienced. What was she doing with her life? What did it mean to be a person of faith in a world that abused their fellow humans so badly? What did the Catholic Church have to say about these immediate issues challenging so many? Underneath it all was the sense, growing stronger by the minute, that if she wanted to be faithful to Jesus, then she would need to follow and pursue the people Jesus loved. And in her heart of hearts, she knew that Jesus was obsessed with the poor—considering them both comrades and friends.

The march on Washington ignited a spark within Dorothy. Like so many people, she was forced to ask herself some hard questions about what her chosen religion had to say to the disinherited of the earth: "I watched that ragged horde and thought to myself: these are Christ's poor. He was one of them. He was a man like other men, and he chose his friends among the ordinary workers."[5] She described how these men felt as if Christianity as a religion and an institution had betrayed them, and she agreed. Perhaps she was thinking about the Founding Fathers immortalized in white marble at the nation's Capitol, the pseudo-Christian language surrounding the myth of America—an America that had failed so many people. Perhaps she was thinking about the priests who told hungry people to pray harder, to be better, and maybe they would be blessed. She saved her real wrath not for the communists but for the religious folks who did nothing to step in and help the working man. "Men are not Christian today," she said, recalling her time at the hunger march. "If they were, this sight would not be possible.

Far dearer in the sight of God are these hungry ragged ones, than all those smug, well-fed Christians who sit in their homes cowering in fear about the Communist menace."[6]

In her questions and anger at religion, an old part of herself had been found and returned to her. And yet she also felt miserably stuck. As I read her words and saw the return to her fiery leftist roots, I sensed the loneliness of a new convert facing the contradictions of putting her faith in action. Her heart was at odds with itself, but what is so beautiful to me about Dorothy Day's story is how she questioned, interrogated, and ultimately asked God for help in resolving this swirl of questions inside of her. She did not have Catholic friends she could go to for advice. She did not have a strong spiritual community outside of the books she read, where, in her mind, Thomas A. Kempis and St. Therese of Lisieux were her best friends—but they were not as practical for real-time and real-life issues in front of her.

She knew what her communist and leftist friends would advise: forget about God and come join the people. This was something her God-haunted heart simply could not do. But in seeing a vision of the face of Christ in the men marching for basic human rights, she thought perhaps there was a place where she could go to for solace, kinship, and possibly even direction.

On the day after the hunger march ended and the people slowly went back to their lives, waiting and hoping for a better world for them and their families, Dorothy went to the National Shrine in Washington, DC to pray on the Feast of the Immaculate Conception. Today, the National Shrine is the largest Catholic church building in America. But in 1932, it was several years old and just beginning to show its potential as a place of pride for Catholics around the United States.

I imagine what the church that she entered was like, before the basilicas were built, with only the ground-floor crypt church built and one small chapel with a shrine to Mary, the mother of God. This is where Dorothy went to pray.[7] Kneeling before the Mother to whom millions around the world looked for solace, kneeling before the woman who knew what suffering was like and who promised her children that one day it would all be redeemed, Dorothy prayed. She asked for a sign. Please, she begged Mary. Show me a way forward. Open up some way for me to work for the poor and the oppressed. And the day she got home to New York was the day she met Peter Maurin.

After Dorothy left DC and returned home to New York City and to Tamar, something troubled and excited her spirit. When she reached her tenement apartment building, she found an older, rumpled man with crooked glasses on his face waiting for her. His suit of clothes was shoddy, pockets crammed with papers; he talked in rhymes and slogans about demanding a better world. She learned he only owned the possessions on his body and didn't have more than a nickel to his name. He looked, in other words, much like the men Dorothy had just seen at the march.

Dorothy didn't know it yet, but that was the day everything changed for her, the day her prayers had been answered. And as usual with Dorothy, it would take a long time to fully understand the miracle of what happened next.

PART 2

THE BIRTH OF THE CATHOLIC WORKER

MEETING PETER MAURIN

The story of the Catholic Worker begins with Peter.
If it were not for Peter there would be no houses
of hospitality and farming communes. Peter has
changed the lives of thousands of people.

—**Dorothy Day,** *House of Hospitality,* 1939

In December of 1932, Dorothy rushed back home after her time away in DC for the hunger march. She had been "coffined" in a bus for eight hours and longed for quiet and a cup of coffee—and to kiss her daughter, Tamar.

But as she opened the door, besides the usual crew of Tamar, John, and his wife, Tessa, there was an older man sitting patiently in the front living room. If she squinted, Dorothy could have mistaken Peter Maurin for someone in the breadlines or a homeless man knocking on doors, asking for shoes or a bit of food. He was short and broad, a French peasant with a thick accent. Every single pocket of his trousers and jacket was filled to bursting with papers and paperback books.

Peter Maurin came to Dorothy's apartment doorstep after the editor of *Commonweal* sent him in her direction. A "red-headed communist in Union square" also told Peter he would find a common friend in Dorothy. Peter read several articles Dorothy had written and, with his usual mix of generosity of spirit and grandiose ideas, declared that she was the current iteration of the fourteenth-century saint and doctor of the church Catherine of Siena, a woman able to move mountains and shift government politics through her faith and advocacy.

He had the gift of sitting in apartments and on street corners, of waiting patiently for his audience to come to him—and when they did, his patience matched his insistence and vision. When Peter showed up unannounced to meet Dorothy Day the writer, he was told she was traveling. Not dissuaded, he invited himself inside and made himself comfortable. Eventually, he took to following Tessa, John's wife, around, espousing his views on the world and religion as she serenely chopped vegetables for their supper. John was slightly alarmed and worried for his wife and Tamar's safety. He wondered if Peter was a dangerous radical or perhaps not all there mentally. He watched Peter get very excitable when he was intent on indoctrinating them, insistent on his ideas.

If both John and Dorothy had had their way, Peter would have been given soup for dinner and sent out the door. But Tessa, who grew up with both the hospitality and anarchist sensibilities of her Spanish father, was amused as this man quoted her poems about money and society while she stirred the soup. Tessa aimed to treat him with dignity and respect, and so they tried, letting him stay at the house until Dorothy came.

While Peter looked like just another hobo in the Bowery, he was a man trained by a religious teaching order in France who sought to marry Catholic social thought and philosophy with pressing economic issues in Europe. As he wandered the streets of New York City, he was looking for a saint to implement a threefold plan he had envisioned for the healing of the world that included calling people back to the land, creating houses of hospitality for the poor, and hosting roundtable conversations where issues of the day could be discussed by both laborers and academics in a community together.

Dorothy, as a writer and an editor, could help him bring his program to fruition. On his own, shouting out his prose poems in Union Square with the other preachers and agitators, Peter was getting nowhere. Now was the time for a new tactic. Nothing less than a complete undoing of the Industrial Revolution was his goal. He dreamed of a near and dear future where people lived off the land and everyone had meaningful work, where the laborer and scholar came together.

And, together with Dorothy, they would start this revolution by publishing a paper for the person in the street.

All of this—the three-part plan to change the world, Dorothy as a saint for the times, the newspaper to be created—Peter excitedly told to Dorothy on that first night. She listened with one ear, her eyes looking longingly at her bed. She was exhausted, skeptical, and consumed with worries about her child and finishing up various freelance projects she needed to complete to pay the rent. She waited until it was late and then gently sent Peter Maurin back into the streets, where he would find a bed somewhere for a quarter. She was relieved that she had done her Christian duty. What she didn't know was that he would show up again the next day. And the next. His persistence and force of conviction both exhausted and charmed her.

"Crackpots with plans to change the social order were a dime a dozen in Union Square during those days," Dorothy always said. But the more she listened to Peter's long, rambling, poetic monologues, the more she understood his unique sensibilities. She saw in him someone who not only complemented her and her background but who could also help her move forward in her faith.

For all of her experiments in poverty, Dorothy was a middle-class, well-educated white woman from a Protestant background. As a child, whenever she showed interest in the Catholic religion, her lapsed-Episcopalian father would scold her, *"That's the church of police officers and Irish washer-women, poor people, and immigrants."* For her, those were words of invitation, and the more she was drawn to issues of poverty, the more she saw the Catholic Church as the religion of the poor.

In the 1930s, even as she attended Mass throughout the week, Dorothy remained an outsider to the worlds she wanted to be a part of: both that of the common laborer and the devout Catholic. Peter was different in so many ways: he grew up poor (born into a large family of peasant farm workers in France, sharing their house with their animals), and he was a Catholic well versed in the intricacies of papal encyclicals and the history of the Church in Europe. She soon realized he was the teacher she had never even known she needed, even if he was a rather odd character.

As Peter continued to show up at her tenement apartment and talk about capitalism and Catholicism, Tamar came down with a case of the measles. Dorothy worriedly sat by her daughter's bed, nursing her back to health, as Peter, nonplussed, would corner the family doctor, who came in to check on Tamar, "hoping to convert a stray apostle," as Dorothy put it. In the days and weeks that followed, Tamar slowly got better but was confined to her bed. Dorothy got her several kittens to play with, and their tenement apartment band grew with the number of people and animals who found shelter there. Dorothy, Tamar, the cats; Tessa, John, and their soon-to-be-born child; and now Peter Maurin, all in one long and narrow apartment. A strange and slightly chaotic family, similar to their neighbors, whose own apartments were full to bursting with a rotating cast of characters in need as well.

Dorothy, with kittens and deadlines always underfoot, began to look differently at Peter the more she listened to his monologues. This man, who only owned the clothes on his back and had a million things to say about the state of the world, was a divine revelation. Perhaps she had been, like the New Testament Book of Hebrews noted, entertaining an angel unaware—an angel with rumpled clothing and a pocket full of sing-song essays. One who looked just like the neighbors lining up and down the streets, looking for a hot meal. One who maybe, just maybe, was an answer to her prayers.

Day after day, Peter showed up to her apartment. He would wait patiently until Dorothy stopped her freelance work—either researching at a public library or banging on her typewriter in the communal kitchen—at around 3:00 p.m. Then he would launch into whatever topic of the day he was interested in. Around ten at night, Dorothy would kick him out and crawl into the tiny bed she shared with Tamar directly behind the kitchen. Peter would spend the night in a bed on the Bowery or sleep on park benches and get a cup of coffee from whatever breadline was available. Then the next day, he would show up at the apartment and wait patiently for his turn for Dorothy's ear and attention.

What impressed Dorothy immediately was Peter's refusal to speak ill of other people. The nearest he ever came to being critical, she said, was in reference to Dorothy herself. He was dismayed by her lack of knowledge of Catholicism. He lectured her about Catholic history and the papal encyclicals, and Dorothy was thrilled to discover that the pope and his curia for some time were writing about labor issues.[1] Peter was grandly ecumenical—among his friends were Jews, Protestants, agnostics, and Catholics—and he found a shared yearning and language in what Catholic social teaching called the "common good." Dorothy later reflected that among these disparate groups, Peter "ignored differences to stress concordance." He viewed anyone who wanted to work toward a better world for the common person as someone on the same team. His mind, body, and spirit were obsessed with the sense of our shared humanity and how to make the world a little better

today, right now. He returned frequently to an old labor slogan—
he wanted, he said, "to build a new society in the shell of the old."
In all earnestness, he told Dorothy he wanted to create a society
in which it is easier for people to be good—good to one another.
People who had their basic needs met and did not have to live in
survival mode, he believed, would find it easier to treat each other
well.

To Peter, working for the common good, creating a new society, and making it easier for people to be good to each other all fit
squarely within his understanding of the rich history of Catholic tradition. This was profoundly exciting for Dorothy. Was God
really good news for the poor? Did Jesus really have anything to
say to the workers who were fasting and marching and being brutalized by the police for basic human rights? Was there a way to be
Catholic and respond to the issues of the day?

Yes, yes! Peter told her that God was close to the workers,
and God wanted a better world for them. And to be Catholic is to
believe that we carry the responsibility in the here and now to care
for our brothers and sisters and to change society to better love our
neighbors. Dorothy couldn't contain her joy. The good news really
was good news for her neighbors, after all.

When Dorothy later told the story of the founding of the
Catholic Worker, she was adamant in pointing to Peter
Maurin, even as people time and time again were drawn to Dorothy herself: her severe nature, her beautiful and alive writing, her
disarming sense of humor and interest in every single person, her

love of good literature and music, her incredibly difficult positions on ethics and war and poverty, her striking looks.

But in her retellings of the birth of the Catholic Worker movement—the paper, the houses of hospitality crammed with people, the back-to-the-land farms and communes that sprung up like mushrooms around the world—Dorothy always pointed to Peter Maurin as the originator. He was the heart and brains of the operation, and Dorothy the practical and shrewd brawn. There was little doubt to those around them that these two illustrious, beautiful, odd people were in a strangely symbiotic relationship. One could not fully succeed without the other.

At the time Peter approached Dorothy, he brought years of both education and manual labor in his bones. Clearly intelligent, Peter had experienced a ramshackle life and was in Canada on a homestead when his farming partner was killed in a logging accident.[2] Moved by this grief, Peter became a wanderer, slipping away from the conventions of the world as he grew older, riding trains in the United States, and living the life of a hobo at times. He taught French but soon stopped taking payment for his tutoring. He gave away all his possessions and would give you the only jacket he owned if you would ask. "The coat you have hanging in your closet belongs to the poor," he would tell you. He lived off of one bowl of soup a day and spent his evenings sleeping in the lodging houses. He believed that if only he could get the ear of priests and bishops, he could ignite a change in how the Church responded to the evils of the age—specifically the economic depression and the lack of employment. His deep love of theology, history, and the Catholic Church animated and undergirded his thoughts to the point that it was all he could talk about—to whomever would listen. He exasperated most people who met him, including Dorothy. He simply could not keep quiet about his ideas, ever.

Since Peter ingratiated himself into their small apartment, Dorothy tried to lay down some ground rules. Among them, if she turned on the radio to listen to a concert broadcast, she would sternly tell Peter that he needed to be quiet and listen. For a while, he would try. Eventually, he would scoot his chair closer to the more empathetic Tessa and whisper urgently in her ear about the evils of industrialization while Dorothy glared at him across the living room. Dorothy was mother, pupil, friend, comrade, and sister to him, sometimes all at the same time. He didn't seem to mind. Once the door to her apartment had been opened to him, Peter managed to squeeze his way in repeatedly. Though just like a cat, he couldn't be counted on to remain long in one place.

Without Dorothy putting his work and insight into the *Catholic Worker* paper, translating his all-over-the-place ideas into something practical, few of us would know about Peter Maurin. I think Dorothy knew this, which is why she wrote about him so much. I think Dorothy also saw in Peter the reality of how the world works: how ignored and despised so many people were. How, in the breadlines, among the rows of shabbily dressed men waiting patiently for their hunger to be filled, lived saints and poets and philosophers who would die unknown in their glory to everyone except Christ. In some ways, I see in Dorothy's retelling of the Catholic Worker movement a desperate sense to give these unknown saints their fair due. Peter Maurin became the pinnacle of this reality for her. He was her own Saint Francis, a man wandering the streets of the Bowery in Lower East Side New York, his head in the clouds with the birds.

All of Peter's ideas—roundtable discussions, houses of hospitality, communal farms—would eventually be put into word and practice as Dorothy brought them to civic gatherings, neighborhood settings, churches, and the *Catholic Worker* newspaper. In the ensuing decades, she met with varying degrees of success—and also abject failure. Peter, in a sense, was the archetype of the "holy fool," and as such would not be bothered by the progress reports in the least. He was someone who the more he tried to understand God, the less he seemed able to fit in with a rapidly changing age that dehumanized people at every turn. He was full to the brim with the poetry of a God who cares for the deep humanity of every person. "They say that I am crazy because I refuse to be crazy the way other people are crazy," he wrote.[3]

What many could not see past in Peter, Dorothy was able to embrace as holy, made in the Divine image of God. And he did the same for her, both of them modeling what radical acceptance of imperfect people can look like. He called her his Catherine of Siena, a saint for the times to move the powers that be. Dorothy scoffed at this, but she was also sharp and pragmatic. As a nonconformist from the start, she knew that the world has always looked to and revered a few strong and genre-bending women—even within the Church. The world was content to let there be a few women to idolize from a safe distance, confident they are the exception to the rule. Dorothy knew this and lived uneasily with this burden, saw the pedestal being built around her. But if she could convince people to see the saintliness of everyone, of every single person, perhaps she could undermine the narrative of the solitary female saint. To do this, she would need help. Dorothy decided, just a few short weeks after meeting him, that Peter Maurin was a holy fool sent to change the world. And she was determined to make that happen.

A LITTLE RED NOTEBOOK, A LITTLE STICK OF DYNAMITE

If the Catholic Church
is not today
the dominant social dynamic force,
it is because Catholic scholars
have failed to blow the dynamite
of the Church.
Catholic scholars
have taken the dynamite
of the Church,
have wrapped it up
in nice phraseology,
placed it in an hermetic container
and sat on the lid.
It is about time
to blow the lid off
so the Catholic Church
may again become
the dominant social dynamic force.

—Peter Maurin

When Dorothy Day was a young child, her most precious possession was a little red notebook wherein she journaled her thoughts—her "only comfort" as a child. She wrote in her notebook to explore her inner world and to make sense of what she noticed about the way society was ordered. From her youngest days, Dorothy wrote to ward off the loneliness that followed her throughout her life. Although her personality attracted many to her—from famous playwrights to down-and-out union men to idealistic young people—she always felt estranged from others in some way.

Her deep desire to live a life of gratitude to God, as the creator of the world, always conflicted with her astute observations of neighbors constantly being exploited. The tensions this created—her belief in a good and present God and the absence of justice and equality in the world—created an internal storm. She was curious and awake and refused to numb herself from asking the questions the psalmists and prophets and poets of the Scripture always seemed to ask: Why is the world the way it is? She loved the earth and humanity so much that it pained her to see suffering.

Her little red journal housed her early thoughts, and eventually all sorts of newspapers held her writings as she sought to make sense of the world. While many people view Dorothy Day as a Catholic activist, she believed her primary vocation was that of a writer. In her lifetime, she published over one thousand articles, wrote multiple books, corresponded constantly through letters, and kept a diary. Millions upon millions of words. Her vivid, vibrant writing style reflected the cultural moments and transcended it, for over six decades.

Historian Mel Piehl traces the themes of Dorothy's hallmark style of muckraking journalism as containing "an obsession with the facts of poverty in affluent America, a personal willingness to share the circumstances of the deprived, and the need to communicate her findings and feelings to a wide public." Until the *Catholic Worker* newspaper, Piehl notes, the missing element in this mix was Dorothy's religious heart.[1] She did not know how to convey her religious impulses and love and faith in God to a wider world. And when she wrote for Catholic magazines, she felt constrained, leaving out her affinity for radical thought and her intellectual wrestlings. In neither context could Dorothy be fully Dorothy on the page, nor could she ever truly write out her inner loneliness. Until, that is, she started the *Catholic Worker*. When Dorothy finally started her own newspaper and wrote what was exactly in her heart, her light was a beacon for those bobbing in the storm-tossed waves of America in the Great Depression. Soon, all sorts of pilgrims gravitated toward her words, and they gravitated toward her light.

It's no surprise, then, that the first element of Peter Maurin's vision to change the world would center around Dorothy's writing. From the first evening they met, Peter brought up the idea of starting a newspaper and "kept harping on it, day after day."[2] Peter loved the idea of schools of perpetual conversation and conversion—roundtable discussions on the issues of the day. It's easy to see how Dorothy was drawn to similar ideas as a young woman— wasn't this what she and the other poets and playwrights were doing in the Hell Hole a decade before? In 1933, in the throes of the Great Depression, after World War I, and with the Third Reich and fascism on the rise in Europe, there were multiple pressing issues to be talked about. The men in Union Square did this all day, and Peter wanted to organize and center the discussion in Catholic social teaching.

Early on, Dorothy seemed to sense the limits of Peter's vision of these roundtable discussions—which also, incidentally, involved him being one of the main speakers: Peter talking in his thick French accent for hours, barely stopping to pause for breath for fear someone would interrupt him. Dorothy simply didn't warm to the idea. She was used to men who had a point to make doing just the same thing: shouting their ideas over the voices of others, a clamor of ideas and posturing. Bringing Union Square soapboxes to tenement apartments didn't appeal to Dorothy's sense of commonality or shared conversation. Her diary entries from the 1930s are filled with stories of men like this—men who talked, talked, talked all day long, regardless if anyone was listening, about how to change the world.

Peter loved to indoctrinate but knew the limitations of it. Born into a culture that prioritized orality and recitation instead of literary pursuits, he only started to write down his thoughts and prose poems later in life. Dorothy's brother John nicknamed these poems "Easy Essays." They became a hallmark of the newspaper, with one or more printed in each issue. Poor Peter couldn't get enough people to listen to his voice in Union Square, but in print, Dorothy amplified the reach he so desperately wanted.

Aware of the issues of the day and the pulse of the speakers in Union Square, Dorothy understood how propagandists indoctrinated others. The square was full of communists hawking their tabloid paper, the *Daily Worker,* related to the issues of the day. She lamented that expressions of their solidarity with the poor came with the message that religion was an enemy. But Dorothy was sharply aware of the successful tactics the communists used—they acknowledged the brokenness of the world, told the suffering man that he deserved better, and assured people that only the communists were working to organize with various groups to build up effective coalitions for change. As they worked hard to get those disenfranchised to join their party, she saw them also taking people away from the Church. And one of the ways they most effectively did all this was through their newspaper.

As Peter taught Dorothy about the papal encyclicals, Catholic history, and European literature, she was deeply impressed. She also quickly understood he wasn't exactly a conversation partner. Teachers teach, Peter would tell her, and his philosophy of teaching included the rhetorical flourish of constant repetition. He was always looking for ways to expand his audience. While he suggested to Dorothy that they start a newspaper, what he had in mind was a scheme for Dorothy to edit and print up his own Easy Essays and nothing else. But Dorothy's mind went to the *Daily Worker* and its successful model of reaching people. An idea was born: she would take Peter's strength of vision and moral clarity and turn it into a tabloid newspaper that focused on the issues of the day but from a Catholic social teaching perspective.

Not many people in the world can sit down to a typewriter and singlehandedly hammer out an eight-page paper taking on the issues of the day with a religious bent, but Dorothy Day knew she could. As she listened to Peter's recitations and essays, she knew she could create a newspaper marrying big ideas of Catholic theology and the history behind it with her best muckraking journalism on her passion topics of labor and injustice.

She knew there was nothing like it in existence, and perhaps there would be no real readership. Perhaps they would be laughed out of the square. Perhaps the Catholic readers she hoped to stir up into justice work would ignore or chastise her. But no matter, she would write the kind of paper she most wished to see in the world. Together, she and Peter would will it into existence—a terrifying, exhilarating, and faith-filled act. It was this wholehearted approach to the *Catholic Worker* that made it an almost instant success.

There was nothing like it in the world, until suddenly it appeared. A miracle decades in the making. The words poured forth out of her like water, her thoughts and insights and longings that previously she poured into her little red notebook, now being printed for all the world to see.

It's important to remember that at this point in the 1930s, many Catholics felt like outsiders in the US religious landscape, where Protestantism was in a position of power. Catholicism was often denigrated as the religion of the poor immigrants flocking to New

York City from Italy and Ireland. While Protestantism enjoyed a cozy relationship with power from the beginnings of the American "experiment," Catholicism had been vilified and pushed to the sidelines. Due to this outsider status, there was little of a radical left presence of Catholicism in the 1930s; instead, many Catholics were pushing for insider status in the hopes of being perceived as "normal" middle-class Americans.

In contrast, different streams of Protestantism, which enjoyed much larger numbers and a wider theological spectrum of difference, had been involved in the social justice gospel movement for multiple decades. Among those streams, the most notable were social gospel movements and Black Protestants advocating for a holistic and liberating gospel centered on the work of Jesus and committed to tearing down structures of white supremacy, including economic systems that oppressed people.

In her first years after she converted, Dorothy wondered how her writing fit into Catholicism as a whole. She regularly went to one priest as her confessor and tried to talk to him about her writing. "I see little of Christ and much of the self in your writing," the priest told her. As Dorothy, in a new faith, sought direction from a spiritual authority, she was almost tempted to receive this advice and correction and humble herself to give up writing altogether. Except that the priest decided he could use Dorothy as a mouthpiece. "I will tell you what to write," he announced to her, confident she would obey him.

She did not, nor did she want to be a mouthpiece for the Church leaders. She also noticed how her confessor was mainly troubled by her writings on social issues. This particular priest was of the opinion it was too late to effect any change in the world and one must focus on preparing for death and the afterlife alone—the very opposite of Dorothy Day's view of religious life.

"Thank God one can change one's confessor," Dorothy later wrote. And I imagine her wicked grin as she did. She went on to find the priest who would become her beloved confessor, Father Zachary, who did not tell her to stop writing but did tell her that she was a terrible writer—"no style, too grim, too realistic." She recalls these experiences with humor, but her comments also relate how the spiritual authorities she voluntarily placed herself under didn't truly recognize her gifts—a theme that would persist all her life (and beyond).

When she was young, Dorothy wrote her questions and sharp observations about the world and about loneliness in her notebook. As she grew older, her questions became more pointed, related both to the suffering she observed and to being a part of a religious institution. How can a faith that makes us more aware of a divine and loving presence in the world also be used as a tool of amnesia, oppression, and consumerism? How can the foundational elements of Christianity—loving God and loving our neighbor—get so twisted and misused to the point where we oppress each other in the name of religion? What does religion have to say to those who are suffering, here and now?

Like an angel, Peter Maurin showed up and told her that the issues of the day affecting the common worker did matter to God. And beyond that, it had mattered to the historic Catholic Church for centuries. Of course, the values had been twisted by human sinfulness, industrialization, capitalism, war, national politics, and more. But core Catholic social teaching prioritized the beloved-ness and the image of God in each and every person and the belief that we are connected and responsible to each other through the mystical body of Christ. Peter said that Catholicism showed the world that charity is the responsibility of the Church, not solely of governments. That we are to address the concrete needs of our neighbors here and now and work for a society that prioritizes those who are the furthest away from flourishing. Through Peter's monologues and the essays he pulled from his pockets, always shoving them at her, Dorothy realized he was the answer to her prayer. An angel in an old shoddy suit who reminded her, over and over again, that she was a cherished comrade in the fight against the constant dehumanization of God's beloved people. That she was a part of a larger religious framework built around this fight—and that she was not alone.

In her little red journals, this was always her greatest fear. Could it be she was the only one who walked the streets of Chicago and could not look away from the scenes of poverty, the smells of the meat-packing industry? She couldn't be the only one horrified by the state of the world, could she? Peter showed her that she wasn't alone. And through his beautiful, complicated mind, he gave her the tools to finally be confident enough in her hopes and dreams for a better world. He gave her the dynamite of the social teachings of the Church; he whispered to her that if we only believed truly in the goodness of God and in our personal responsibility to our neighbor, the whole world as we know it would be upended.

Dorothy listened to his dreams reflecting her own and knew she had to do something. So she sat down at her typewriter and lit a match.

MAY DAY

For those who are sitting on park benches in the warm spring sunlight. For those who are huddling in shelters trying to escape the rain. For those who are walking the streets in the all but futile search for work. For those who think there is no hope for the future, no recognition of their plight—this little paper is addressed. It is printed to call their attention to the fact that the Catholic Church has a social program—to let them know there are men of God who are working not only for their spiritual but their material welfare.

—**"To Our Readers,"** from the first issue of the *Catholic Worker*, May 1933

I was all for plunging right in. After all, I had a typewriter and a kitchen table and plenty of paper and plenty to write about.

—**Dorothy Day**, On Loaves and Fishes

Dorothy Day came from newspaper people—her father and two older brothers were in the business—but all three of them were nonreligious and staunchly conservative. Dorothy had the skills of reporting and editing to fall back on from her own past, but to go from freelance writing to publishing an eight-page tabloid newspaper from her kitchen table was a big step. At first, she clung to Peter's proclamations that producing the newspaper would be a group effort. But when she asked him how they were going to go about doing it—getting the money for the printers, writing up and editing the copy—Peter did not even pretend to be practical. "I enunciate the principles," he told her with a grandiose air about him, leaving everything else squarely on her shoulders. "But where do we get the money?" Dorothy asked him, her stomach sinking as she realized Peter's role involved theories but not systems, production, or fundraising. When she sought practical advice, Peter would meet it by launching into a lecture on the history of saints in the Catholic Church and how they always raised the capital necessary for their efforts through prayer: "God sends you what you need when you need it. You will be able to pay the printer—just read the lives of the saints."

Dorothy both despaired and marveled at the hubris of this man. She did not have time to immerse herself in the lives of the saints as she now was tasked with doing all the practicalities of the paper herself as a single mother in the midst of the Great Depression. But as much as Peter annoyed her, she also found his childlike faith in God providing to be truly inspirational. *Loaves and fishes, loaves and fishes,* Peter told Dorothy. If you let yourself get to a place of being hungry, belly empty, desperate for some sustenance,

God was sure to send someone with loaves and fishes to share with you. God would be in charge of getting the message out, he said, of multiplying their little offering.

Dorothy looked at her crowded kitchen table and saw it could be the editorial offices of a small newspaper. John could help edit, and Tamar and Peter could pass out the paper in Union Square. With a little bit of prayer and a lot of imagination, why couldn't it all happen here, and why couldn't it be now?

Peter had told Dorothy that he knew a church where perhaps the newspaper offices could be in the basement, and he promised Dorothy the priest would be able to front the money for printing. Even though she hadn't known him long, Dorothy was already aware of how the "saintliness" of Peter could make him an unreliable narrator when it came to the practical things of life. The parish priest never came through with money for the first edition of the paper, nor were any offices ever offered up.

Dorothy herself found a printer and got a printing quote for 2,500 copies of an eight-page newspaper: fifty-seven dollars. Too impatient to wait for God to drop the money in her lap from the sky, she decided instead to take her earnings from her most recent freelance articles and simply pay the printer instead of paying the rent or electricity for her apartment. Whether she told John and Tessa about this plan is unclear. Nor did the income from the paper make good financial sense. She already knew she wanted to sell it for a penny a copy so it could be affordable to the men in the streets. So even if she sold every single copy, that would bring in less than half of the cost of printing the paper.

Perhaps Dorothy was more like Peter than she realized, because she charged full speed ahead with this plan, knowing she would be working round the clock to report, write, and edit the paper and also lose money with each issue.

On the front page of the first issue were two workers on the masthead—one with a pickax and one with a mallet. The headlines were in bold font: "Easy Essays," "The Listener," "Negro Labor on Levees Exploited by the US War Dept.," "Less Child Labor Due to Present Low Wage Scale." There was also, near the bottom of the front page, a simple box filled with the words "Do Something! Join the Catholic League for Social Justice Now!"[1] Dorothy was pulling out all the stops: getting people's attention and then telling them to "do something" by joining in with her work (grandly calling it the Catholic League for Social Justice before it eventually just became the Catholic Worker community).

With her first editorial, Dorothy laid all of her cards on the table: "It is time there was a Catholic paper printed for the unemployed. The fundamental aim of radical sheets is to convert people to radicalism and Atheism. Is it not possible to be a radical and not be atheist? Is it not possible to protest, expose, to complain, to point out abuses and demand reforms without desiring the overthrow of religion?"

Her answer was a resounding yes. And she spent all eight pages of her tabloid newspaper doing just what she said she would: exposing, complaining, pointing out abuses, and demanding change—all from the framework of a good and pious Catholic woman. She knew she would confuse people, and a part of me thinks that she relished this element of her paper. Out of Dorothy poured a jam-packed paper full of the hot-button stories of the day, most of them related to issues of work and labor in a country several years into the worst economic recession in its history. Among the article topics included in the first issue alone were:

- school strikes
- the exploitation of Black workers by the US government
- child labor and the record-low wages of 1933
- issues of women in the textile industry and how they could organize for better conditions
- an in-depth look at the Scottsboro Boys trial and the nuances of the case
- theological reflections on racism from a priest
- various labor strikes
- journalistic pieces on unemployment
- first-person essays noting the conditions of poverty in the neighborhood in families and among young working women
- various book reviews

Scattered throughout were various quotes by popes and priests, and nods to papal decrees and encyclicals that shored up her arguments (all of which was informed by Peter Maurin).

Every element and article was carefully thought out by Dorothy. Every piece was written, selected, and edited by her, with help from her brother John. The first issue was scheduled to be released on May

Day 1933, a day meant to commemorate the issues of the working class and labor rights worldwide. Her editorial was meant to be read by both the common man in Union Square and the cardinal of New York City, with something within from which they both could learn.

Dorothy also chose to dedicate the first issue of the *Catholic Worker* to the police, who had a history of treating organized workers brutally and who also tended to be Catholic. On the bottom of the front page it read, "This first issue of THE CATHOLIC WORKER is dedicated to the police of New York City, who we expect to be out in great numbers on May Day and whose attention we wish to call to the two encyclicals, The Reconstruction of the Social Order, by Pope Leo XIII, and Forty Years After, by Pope Pius XI. If the police don't want to buy this paper we will give it to them. As so many of them are good Catholics, prominent and resplendent in Holy Name Processions and at Communion breakfasts, we feel sure that they will give this issue, which is dedicated to them, their sympathetic and intelligent attention."

In its wickedly cheeky dedication, it points to the general approach Dorothy was bound and determined to take: No "good Catholics" were off limits in her paper. Frank discussions of systemic injustice and current issues playing out in her city would be addressed, constantly. By this point in her life, Dorothy herself had been imprisoned two times and treated brutally by the US justice system, so when she writes about the police that "so many of them are good Catholics," it's almost painfully sharp. Catholics, she insists, can be a part of social justice movements, but first she must also address how "good" Catholics have been at the forefront of the suppression of justice.

In a time when issues of racism, police brutality, economic inequality, and rampant individualism continue to make the headlines, and people of faith, both Protestant and Catholic alike, struggle to understand how to confront unjust systems, Dorothy's first issue of the *Catholic Worker* is a revelation. Even in her simple dedication to the NYPD, she is fully herself: funny, irreverent, religious, and painfully sad all at once. But more than anything, it is brilliant. By dedicating the issue to the police (and bossily asking them to read almost forty thousand words of the pope's addresses on labor issues as homework), she is demanding their engagement. And, she sweetly adds, if they are unwilling to pay the penny a copy price, she will gladly give it to them for free.

We who want justice can be fully ourselves as well: we can demand another world for our neighbors but have a sense of humor about it. We can accept that we live in an imperfect system and point out the hypocrisies as we see them. We can be passionate about equality and enjoy what little strides are made forward. We can be both spiritually devout and constantly horrify our fellow religious folks. Because underneath it all, we must see ourselves as Dorothy saw the world: truly joined and connected to each other. She was poking fun at the police, calling them out for their violence, but truly wanted them to engage with the issue and change their hearts and policies. If the police could see the world as she did, as she believed God did, then the world would be better for everyone. But this doesn't mean she always had to be polite about it.

One of the things I love most about Dorothy is how she publicly scolded prominent religious people right out of the gate. It was not only the police, but also near the end of the first issue she lampoons the mayor of New York City. Mayor O'Brian, a well-known Catholic, had recently attended a prominent prayer breakfast in the city, where he told people in light of the Great Depression to "pray and pray and pray. That will make our people happy and bring our people back to prosperity again." Dorothy points out that O'Brian's pious instructions to simply pray harder instead of changing the social order recalled a chant that was popular with anarchists and communists who saw right through religious ruses: "work and pray and live on hay, when you die you'll get pie in the sky."[2]

This chant was close to Dorothy's heart because it was a slap in the face to the powerful religious people—those who focused on the afterlife to get out of caring for their neighbors in the present. She understood the anger communists and leftists alike felt at Catholics like the mayor and the police because she herself burned from within at the hypocrisy of her chosen religion. It was a struggle that remained with her all her life and infused her writing with a particular kind of poignancy. She was desperate for Catholics to live up to their stated ideals.

The question Dorothy continued to ask herself and others was: how can one be a Catholic in the world when the most prominent and visible Catholics had nothing to say to the working-class men and women who were struggling in overwhelming numbers? Her answer through the *Catholic Worker* was to make it plain that there were other ways of being Catholic in the world and that the current expressions of apathetic faith were in direct opposition to the teachings of Christ. And thanks to Peter Maurin and his encyclopedic knowledge of Catholic history and social teachings, she could now prove it.

With every issue, with every article about injustice and exploitation, every engagement with Catholics both high and low, Dorothy created pathways for people of faith to view their involvement in social issues and direct social action as a historic component of their religion. Like Peter Maurin always talked about, she tried to make a world where it was easier to be good. And sometimes, she knew, you had to do a bit of muckraking to make such a world possible.

On May Day 1933, Union Square was teeming with men— Dorothy wrote that there were two hundred thousand communists and trade union members milling about, preparing to march and demonstrate and celebrate the hard-won labor victories and demand more change.[3] Spring was in full force; there was beer in the streets and change in the air despite the effects of the Great Depression. It was busy, it was raucous, it was a day of immense significance to the working man—perfect, thought Dorothy, for launching her paper. This was the readership Dorothy set her sights on, a crowd itching for a better world immediately. She picked up the bundles of the *Catholic Worker* from the printer, and then she, Tamar, and three Catholic boys sent by a local priest plunged into the crowd of men in the square, shouting out the headlines and masthead: "Come get the *Catholic Worker,* a cent a copy!"

As they called out to sell the paper, people were intrigued, confused, annoyed. "A Catholic paper? Are you kidding me?" was the most common response. They received jeers, shouts, and hostility. Two of the boys sent to help fled, even as the remaining one brave soul gritted his way through the day, trying to sell the paper. But Dorothy kept going. She knew if these men actually read her paper, many would be on her side.

By all accounts, she wasn't bothered by the men in Union Square who expressed bafflement, mirth, even contempt for her and her paper. She wasn't going anywhere, and what copies of the *Catholic Worker* she didn't sell on the street she postmarked and sent off to parishes around New York City and beyond. She wanted both her neighbors lining up for the breadlines and the important bishops of her city to read her paper. But more than a readership, which she eventually got, what Dorothy wanted most was to actually change the world.

I think about how Dorothy used that chant in her first issue, *work and pray and live on hay, and when you die, you'll get pie in the sky.* How she was saying this is how the working class, the unemployed, and the exploited have observed religion, from time immemorial. Dorothy agreed with them and felt that they rightly rejected a faith that had nothing to offer earthly suffering. Dorothy knew the chant was true, that it spoke to the reality of how little Christians had done to end oppression here on earth and how impoverished and ethereal the US Catholic imagination was in 1933. But she also brought something that so few people had at that time: hope that another world was possible. She was a single mother with no money, a fledging Catholic convert, a woman whose apartment was starting to become overrun with people with no homes or shoes or coats or food, a woman who filled her head with books but had few people with whom to converse about them—and was filled to the brim with a radical hope that the world could change in her lifetime.

To be more specific, Dorothy Day had hope that people of faith, Catholic people in particular, could be at the forefront of this change. She herself wanted to read a paper of faith for the unemployed, but it didn't exist. And so she created it, writing every word for herself as much as anyone.

She believed that the love of God found her in the world. She believed that the God who found her was marching in the streets with those demanding rights. She believed Jesus of Nazareth had much more in common with the everyday person in the Great Depression than he did with mayors who attended prayer breakfasts or the faith leaders who led them in prayer instead of leading to change policies.

She had hope in love changing the world. And she published her paper with that stubborn hope shining through in every story, every page, and every quip. It was her tiny spark sent into the world, 2,500 copies she gave out until there was none left. She had no way of knowing how ready the world was for this kind of hope or the kind of good trouble it would get her in. How could she? All she could do was try. Do Something! Join Us! She wrote. She tried to not be shocked when people responded in droves. But she couldn't help it. Her faith was still growing, just like the paper.

GOOD AS BREAD

Why be a liberal when you could be a liberator?

—Peter Maurin, *The Forgotten Radical*

The second Dorothy had given away every issue of the first edition of the *Catholic Worker*, it was time to start planning the next. Dorothy wrote in her book *House of Hospitality* that "while Peter read aloud his inspired lines on hospitality we had as yet no office."[1] Dorothy wrote articles on park benches, editing them at her dining room table while Tamar played with kittens underfoot. She had plenty to say, and so did Peter, but how to sustain it? How to pay for it?

As would become the pattern, her readers showed up for her. One Black priest gave Dorothy ten dollars. A nun sent in one dollar. Various small amounts of money trickled in from readers from Union Square and beyond who were moved by this new project. Donations and letters started to come in from places and parishes Dorothy hadn't even sent her paper. The *Catholic Worker* became the kind of artifact people read and then passed along to others, hand to hand, mind to mind, heart to heart. Somehow, Dorothy was able to pay her rent for the month. Her brother John got a new job and moved out with Tessa and his baby, and at the exact same time, Dorothy decided to also rent the vacant barber shop below her tenement apartment for twenty-five extra dollars a month (she harrumphed that this was a terribly high price to pay for an old place with no heat, but she did it anyway). After the first issue came out, already working on the second one, Dorothy stood downstairs alone and surveyed what she hoped would be the offices of the *Catholic Worker*. It was an empty building, for she owned no office furniture and had even sold her own typewriter in order to pay for the printing of the next issue of the paper. She decided she would pen it by hand until another typewriter showed up. She was beginning to get the hang of the loaves-and-fishes life.

Slowly, the *Catholic Worker* office filled with supplies—a communist friend brought furniture; someone else did indeed donate a typewriter. Unlike Peter, who hated to ask for money and preferred to wait around for miracles, Dorothy didn't have the idealistic luxury of noble poverty. She put needs out there, asking people for money, and often put into subsequent issues of the *Catholic Worker* descriptions of what the needs were.

The way she later told it, the office became a sort of metaphor for the cyclical nature of following Christ: sometimes they would overflow with donations, only to be cleaned out again when a just-evicted family with no belongings came by asking for furniture. Dorothy began her long decades of being dependent on others and being committed to giving away whatever was asked of her. As Dorothy and Peter lived the biblical defintion of charity, a model emerged of following Jesus that meant putting yourself in positions of need and trust. For Dorothy as for Peter, this kind of voluntary poverty held an element of adventure and was a non-negotiable part of life at the Catholic Worker, which was quickly becoming not just an established newspaper—but also movement.

The miracles and sacrifices evened out into a way of living that was chaotic, delightfully countercultural, exhausting, and exhilarating. A slow trickle of people found their way to Dorothy and offered their skills: young college-educated women eager to write and edit, various propagandists who felt they found a home, a handful of immigrants and refugees who needed a safe place to land, young idealists with their heads full of leftist thoughts.

This motley crew helped edit and circulate the paper and beg for resources from whatever place they could. Because of the paper and the growing circle of editors, dreamers, and paper sellers, more and more neighbors started to show up to her ground-floor apartment seeking help. The Great Depression was in full swing, and evictions were a constant. Dorothy and an ever-changing crew of people—the lines blurred between those who came to get help and those who came to give it—started to make sure there was always a pot of coffee and a pot of soup on the stove in the *Catholic Worker* office. The newspaper office now became a hub of community, discussions, need, and neighborliness.

Peter Maurin would be proud, thought Dorothy. But where the hell was he?

A s much as she sometimes tuned out Peter and his constant stream of speech, it turns out that he could misunderstand

Dorothy as well. He didn't like the title of the paper and its allusions to the *Daily Worker*. He hoped the paper would be called the *Catholic Radical*—radical, after all, means "the root," and Peter wanted to make it clear that the Catholic social teachings were indeed the root of the Church. When he read the first issue, he was surprised and disappointed to see all of Dorothy's articles and editorials obsessed with labor issues and inequality in the United States. He didn't like the variety of topics covered in eight pages, declaring that "everybody's paper was nobody's paper."

He was so hurt that he left New York for a month. Dorothy, puzzled by his response, soon realized Peter truly thought the paper would consist of eight pages of his Easy Essays. Dorothy had put several into the paper, putting Peter's name on the masthead as editor (although she misspelled his name, which also offended him), thinking she had fairly acknowledged his contribution to the endeavor.

But Peter, a teacher through and through, focused intently on repeating propaganda in order to bring about change in the social order. Dorothy's slice-of-life stories and muckraking journalistic exposés of labor violations in the United States didn't meet his vision. He didn't think the paper should focus on labor issues at all but instead advocate for a Catholic approach to changing the world, person by person, idea by idea.

Dorothy loved the masses, but Peter loved the Christ who loved the individual, and Peter saw everyone as responsible for doing their part to change the world order, starting from within. He poured his heart into his essays and aimed to reach for the heart of everyone else. In his own childlike way, he believed that if enough people read his essays, the world could change, overnight. But Dorothy knew that for the majority of her audience, they needed a crash course in understanding the issues of social injustice happening in their country in order to spur them on to action. And based on the incredible response to her paper, Dorothy was right.

Peter Maurin, offended, eventually returned to the office only to gravely tell Dorothy to take his name off the editorial masthead of the paper. He would allow her to publish several of his Easy Essays in each issue—he would be a freelance columnist, a troubadour—but he would not align his name with everything else in the paper.

For the next decade or so, this was to be a repeated pattern. Peter Maurin was the idealist with a heart of gold and little interest in anything outside of his plan to change the world for the better. He would live with his bitter disappointments close to the heart, only to eventually come back around to believing in the goodness and possibilities of what could happen next. History is full of examples of people like Peter, with singular ideas and belief in how necessary these ideas are for changing hearts and minds and structures. But there is a cost to living life with such singularity, especially for someone like Dorothy, in relationship with a driven, idealistic person.

Dorothy learned to treat Peter on his own terms, as she did many others who came in and out of her life and her houses of hospitality in the ensuing decades—a gift from God to be welcomed in whatever form they came and for however long they stayed.

Peter would sometimes leave New York City and travel the country, leaving Dorothy and the *Catholic Worker* in the dark as to his whereabouts (sometimes in her columns in the paper, she would write messages to him or plead with him to come back to the offices, which he usually eventually did). When he didn't like something Dorothy published, he would withdraw from her. He often lamented aloud about her female sensibilities, which annoyed her to no end (he often airily said things like "man proposes; women disposes" in regard to his thoughts on the *Catholic Worker* paper), disappointed she wasn't a propagandist and teacher like himself.

Dorothy was nothing if not practical. She liked Peter's personalist approach, but she also agreed with the communists. Capitalism wasn't working, and the widening inequality and suffering as a result of industrialization and exploitation needed addressing. As someone who had long been interested in labor issues, she wanted people, especially Catholics, to get involved in the fight for fair wages and dignifying working conditions immediately.

Since she believed all people were made in the image of God, she wanted an economic and social system that reflected this view better than the current world order. She knew and used the language and tactics of leftist organizers and journalists who pointed out how dehumanizing labor in the United States was. She considered supporting protests and strikes a Christian duty, just as much as going to Mass and praying.

Over and over again, Peter would respond, "Strikes just don't strike me." Without a revolution of the heart, the transforming work of Christ, Peter did not see how the social order could change. But Dorothy believed in seeking agreement around Jesus's words: those who aren't against us are for us.

For Dorothy, that meant co-laborers in the movement were leftists and people involved in the issues of class struggle. "The bottle will still smell of the liquor it once contained," she would say in regard to her socialist and anarchist leanings or her obsession with class war and labor issues that seeped into her writings. Socialists wanted the means of production to go back to the worker and to fight against the concentration and hoarding of wealth by a few. Anarchists wanted to give power back to the individual and did not trust institutions and governments to take care of them, instead incurring personal responsibility and mutual aid and support. Dorothy saw direct connections here to scripture and Christian Catholic teaching.

I love this tension, the ways Dorothy and Peter pushed each other, annoyed each other, disagreed with each other. It takes all kinds of radicals to change the world, and Dorothy knew this intimately. She viewed Peter as the answer to her prayers in the form of inspiration, education, and the kick in the pants to start something. Although Peter was disappointed at times in Dorothy for going outside and beyond his aims, in many ways he continued to view her as an answer to his own prayers as well. Perhaps he was even able to temper his dismay at her incorrigible nature with gentle humor. He himself had helped envision, name, and create an unruly kind of saint: a Catherine of Siena whom he could not control, a woman who was prone to propose and dispose of whatever she liked, regardless of whether or not her miraculous angel Peter Maurin approved.

"Peter was as good as bread," Dorothy wrote in 1963, several years after his death.[2] She didn't agree with how people described him as joyful or cheerful; she instead thought that he was a truly happy man—neither concerned with what worried other people nor consumed by their thoughts. He was free.

He lived his life stubbornly insisting that we should not wholeheartedly embrace the merits of big government, technology, and urbanization.[3] His ethics echoed the way of Jesus and his parables about mustard seeds, grains of yeast, a tiny pearl of great price. Peter's distributism ideas, combined with his obsession with farms and back-to-the-land movements, did not fit neatly into socialist or communist models and raised wonderfully complex questions for people like Dorothy. He would continue to view the voluntary communal, agrarian life as the ultimate goal. A world where everyone could find dignifying labor and where everyone could flourish.

Nearly one hundred years (and over two millennia) later, what is astonishing is how resonant and countercultural these beliefs continue to be. Peter Maurin was a consistent person in Dorothy's life, calling her to consider other ways of thinking beyond the obsession with the eternal now—beyond the ever-present urge to get involved in labor issues, in strikes, to beat the communists at their game.

Perhaps he reflected on his own childhood being raised on a farm, which contained elements of profound joy and connection to both the earth and his fellow humans, and he wanted this for everyone. What must it have been like for him to see the long lines of men in the crowded, filthy cities with no hope of work and for a variety of reasons being cast aside in a society that only valued what you could produce for others?

Peter, good as bread, never stopped hoping another world was possible. And in the meantime, he would do what he could. He would accept each day his daily bread and urge others to do the same. He would expect the loaves and fishes to miraculously appear, for people to come forth of their own accord to give what little they had. And he expected God alone to do the multiplying, to feed the thousands and thousands who so desperately needed it. God had done it before, and God could do it again. All you needed were eyes to see and a stomach hungry enough to care.

HOW PRAYER WORKS

1. People who are in need
and are not afraid to beg
give to people not in need
the occasion to do good
for goodness' sake.
2. Modern society calls the beggar
bum and panhandler
and gives him the bum's rush.
But the Greeks used to say
that people in need
are the ambassadors of the gods.
3. Although you may be called
bums and panhandlers
you are in fact
the Ambassadors of God.
4. As God's Ambassadors
you should be given food,
clothing and shelter
by those who are able to give it.

5. Mahometan teachers tell us
that God commands hospitality,
and hospitality is still practiced
in Mahometan countries.
6. But the duty of hospitality
is neither taught nor practiced
in Christian countries.

—**Peter Maurin**

You pray for the hungry, and then you feed them.
This is how prayer works.

—**Pope Francis**

To anyone he could get to listen, Peter talked about hospitality. He was drawn to ideas about houses of hospitality around the world and in history—including Muslim cultures and Middle Eastern Jewish cultures like those that Jesus was born into. And Dorothy, after living for several years in tenement apartments, recognized that many of her neighbors embedded this way of hospitality in their cultures. The generosity of the laborer and the "common man" continually astounded and ministered to Dorothy, and in them she saw the ways of the saints of the church made real and practical. It was those people like her—middle-class and well-educated—who needed the help of others to live out the values of hospitality and generosity of Christ (a common theme of the stories of Jesus).

Peter espoused the ways throughout history that people had created hospices or places for the stranger, the foreigner, those living in poverty and those who were sick—the vulnerable in society that the Hebrew scriptures talked about constantly. Before "God's preferential option for the poor"[1] became part of official Church teaching, Peter Maurin pointed to those many people of faith who were intrinsically drawn to care for vulnerable people because they sensed God's care and concern for them. In an unequal and unjust society, God's eye was on the poor, and special care should be taken to ensure they were flourishing.

As he lectured and recited his poems on houses of hospitality, Dorothy saw with a flash how Peter's message was perfect for the times they were living through. He taught her the traditional Catholic teachings of the spiritual works of mercy: instruct the ignorant, counsel the doubtful, admonish the sinners, bear patiently those who wrong us, forgive offenses, comfort the afflicted, and pray for the living and the dead. He also taught Dorothy about the corporal, or embodied, works of mercy: to feed those who are hungry, give water to the thirsty, clothe the naked, shelter those with no homes, visit the sick and those imprisoned, and bury the dead. If you do these things to anyone, Jesus said, then you are doing them to me.[2]

You must always do both, side by side, said Peter, the spiritual *and* the embodied works of mercy. This is how you live out your faith on a daily basis. As she listened to Peter, Dorothy was thrilled to discover how all her dreams of making the world a better place were long manifested in Catholic theology. And it couldn't have come at a better time: 1933 was the absolute height of unemployment in the United States, with almost 25 percent of the population unemployed. People were hungry and thirsty; they needed clothes and shelter. They needed care for illness, addiction, mental issues. Dorothy thought about the political prisoners and the women she had met in jail and how little dignity they received, and the people who died alone and penniless. As she looked at her neighbors, her community, the headlines, she recognized people fitting every one of these categories that Jesus gave us, people who needed the works of mercy right that very second. She saw Jesus in the breadlines and in jail and in the houses of ill repute. And she wanted other people to see Jesus in lines, jails, and houses too.

Later, she would slyly say that her writing qualified as a spiritual work of mercy because she was "instructing the ignorant." But the truth is that there was work to be done in sharing Catholic social teachings with her Catholic readers and the necessity of them getting involved in the struggle to take care of their neighbors. There was a growing gap between devout Peter Maurin's ethic of "the coat that hangs in one's closet belongs to the poor" and the average Catholic layperson sitting in the pews, praying for eternal salvation while disregarding the poor (and blaming them for their own problems). Peter's thoughts on hospitality were directly related to voluntary poverty—he advocated for giving away possessions, wealth, and stability as a result of Christian conviction (indeed, he lived and slept in one pair of clothes at all times and would gladly give the coat he was wearing to anyone who asked for it). Voluntary poverty was a historic Christian tradition and something anyone of means could enter into, he thought, and it could actually bring you closer to Christ. Who wouldn't want that?

But it was Dorothy's knack for distilling Peter's passion for people and for truly living like Jesus into a memorable turn of phrase that engaged her readership. She declared that Peter's message of radical hospitality, generosity, and commitment to voluntary poverty was really a form of taking on personal responsibility—for your neighbors, she added, lest the individualist rejoice too quickly. This was not a promotion of the pull-yourself-up-by-your-bootstraps mentality many Americans held but was instead an answer to the age-old question of "Who is my neighbor, and what is my responsibility to them?"

The answer, according to Jesus, was that if someone was in need and you could address that need, it was your responsibility to do so. Both Peter and Dorothy knew that the closer you are to your neighbors in need, the harder it will be to forget your responsibility to them. Which is why she often wrote personal stories illuminating the realities of people in poverty, trying to prick the conscience of those who would rather turn a blind eye to the realities of the unequal and unjust world.

She strove to shine a light on specific injustices against women, children, Black Americans, the Jewish community, the working man, unions, and more. She made the reality of people in poverty come alive for those sitting in their homes and churches across her country. She asked people to care, to have the stories of injustice wound and pierce their hearts. And then she told them to use this wounding to change their lives, to actually do something about social injustice, and to do it in the name of Jesus. And as always, she decided to practice what she preached herself.

As the readership of the paper grew, so did the practical work; more and more people started showing up at her apartment, asking for help. Dorothy was overwhelmed by the needs of her neighbors, especially when it came to housing. In August of 1932, according to the New York Welfare council, there were 420 evictions. By August of 1933, that number had tripled to 1,257 in one month alone.[3] It felt to Dorothy like a never-ending attempt to put out the fires of the economic downturn of the past five years. She helped arrange pushcarts to assist families in moving their belongings after being evicted, offered to help people sign up for the measly relief checks, and sat with the misery of families with nowhere else to go. Living close to the Bowery and the seventeen thousand beds the US government had set up for homeless men seeking work, she daily saw visible misery and hopelessness. She observed the row upon row of men crammed into bunkbeds and eating at long wooden tables, the men in need stretching for two city blocks.[4] It was an excruciating time for her, the needs too big to be filled by her alone.

What made it even harder for Dorothy was the reality that many Catholic bishops and important intellectual and theological minds were starting to get wind of her little project and wanted to learn more.[5] She would rush from trying frantically to keep a family with young children from being put out on the streets only to find a priest waiting to argue with her about communism in her office over a cup of tea.

She started to seize upon an idea Peter had about putting all of these concerned church leaders into action. One of Peter's ideas related to solving the issue of homelessness revolved around the idea of houses of hospitality. He referenced St. Jerome and his advice that every home should have a room set aside for a brother in need—a "Christ's room," as he called it. Peter took this idea further, and in October 1933, he addressed one of his Easy Essays to the bishops on the front page of the *Catholic Worker*. He envisioned houses of hospitality that could be "centers of Catholic Action in every diocese."[6] He wrote, "We need Houses of Hospitality to give to the rich the opportunity to serve the poor. We need Houses of Hospitality to bring the Bishops to the people and the people to the Bishops. . . . We need houses of hospitality to show what idealism looks like when it is practiced."[7] He wanted every Catholic Church in New York City and beyond to start housing those who needed it. Immediately.

Peter's belief in the goodness of people and in the institution of the Catholic Church was so strong that he simply believed it would not be all that long before every parish church sponsored a house of hospitality for those in need, even converting their church buildings and housing for priests into housing for the men and women and children who needed it desperately. He had immense hope that the long lines of suffering men, women, and children in the Bowery would become a relic of a cruder time. It all made so much sense to him. Peter was sure that his beliefs were impeccably aligned with Catholic theology and doctrine, and the vast numbers of people in need in New York City and beyond pointed to the urgency of the moment. If ever the Catholic Church was going

THE BIRTH OF THE CATHOLIC WORKER

to have a day to shine and take care of its neighbors in need, that day was now!

While Peter waited on the Church to show up and live out its stated values, Dorothy was finding it hard to keep her head above water. She was trying to write the paper plus deal with the daily constant stream of visitors and regulars. An unemployed and pregnant young woman came in and "took over the kitchen"; started cooking meals for the homeless men who would wander in. People stopped by for bread or soup and stayed in the kitchen, talking long into the night. Clothing donations were dropped off and given away almost immediately. Soon, due to the volume of people coming in and out, a schedule was arranged, and people ate in shifts in the small kitchen. The intellectual types gathered in the tiny yard and discussed philosophy, while the working-class folks ate their meals and then went out into the streets to sell the *Catholic Worker* paper. The official visiting hours, Dorothy said, were from 8:00 a.m. until midnight, and they tried to keep the soup and coffee going that entire time.[8]

Immediately, Dorothy noted, the class war, or what Peter called the divide between the scholar and the worker, was making itself felt. All the disparate groups of people gathering at her home did not get along. But Peter was delighted by it—"it makes for the clarification of thought," he told Dorothy happily. It was a mix of unemployed and houseless people, friends Peter had made all over the city, various neighbors (some curious, some in need), professors, and theologians—and a crew of regular characters was starting to form.

Impatient with the Church, Dorothy rented an apartment for men with donations that trickled in for the paper (and also housed several people, including Peter Maurin, in her own apartment). Right after establishing a men's house of hospitality, she put out a call in the November issue for fellow Catholics to start houses for unemployed women who found themselves in very precarious situations. She wrote of their heartbreaking conditions—many of these women finding themselves in awful or compromised places, and all they wanted was a safe place and dignifying work.

Again, they were met with silence from the Church leadership. Priests, much to Peter's dismay, were not falling all over themselves to convert their spaces into housing for the homeless. But the hospitality of the poor made itself known—many of the donations for the women's house came from working-class Catholic ladies who had very little extra and yet gave what they had. The widow's mite, coming through again. Dorothy, seemingly writing to herself, said, "To those who are discouraged at the vastness of the work to be done, and the slightness of the work accomplished, we wish to call attention to the fact that if fifty parishes or schools or organizations would enter on a similar work, five hundred women would be taken care of before the winter is out and it can all be done with the fifty-cent, regularly-made donations of working girls and married women themselves."[9]

It wasn't just the donations of the working class that enabled Dorothy to start the second house of hospitality; it was also the severity of the need that pushed her into action. Eileen Eagan tells a story (although it was never written down by Dorothy) about two houseless women who would often come to the Catholic

Worker offices. They were a pair who survived on the streets with each other and came to Dorothy for food and clothes and soup and were hoping for a place to stay. They must have been some of the women Dorothy had in her mind when she was writing her appeals in her newspaper for funds to rent another space. Shortly after the November paper came out, Dorothy was visited by only one of the women who used to come daily. "Where is your friend?" Dorothy asked. The woman somberly told her the story: The previous night, desperate to escape the cold, the women had tried to find shelter in the subway tunnels. Cold and surrounded by dirt, filth, and trash, her companion simply decided she couldn't do it anymore. She threw herself into an oncoming train, ending her misery.[10]

Dorothy decided she was done waiting around for the Church to step up. She threw on a coat and went out and knocked on doors herself, begging parish priests to donate the fifty dollars she would need to rent an apartment. She started housing women without waiting for the donations or indeed any furniture or necessities like blankets. The need was too great, the misery too overwhelming to wait for Christians to do what they were supposed to do.

When Dorothy wrote about how it all came about, she simply said that "the need made itself felt." In her paper, after describing how the house for women only had three beds for fifteen women, Dorothy declared that "the winter is on and we can wait no longer":

> We can borrow blankets for the time being and use those
> of the editors. They can roll themselves in coats and news-
> papers, which are said to be very warm, though we are

sure they are very noisy. However, we hug to ourselves the assurance that all these things, such as blankets, will be added unto us, so we are not dismayed. Come to think of it, there are two rugs on the Catholic Worker floor which, if energetically beat out, will serve as covers. Christ's first bed was made of straw.

This closeness to the tragedy of what it was like to be poor in New York in 1933 absolutely clarified the faith and life of Dorothy Day. It wasn't just one constant stream of miracles, nor did these houses of hospitality—or the shoes, coats, soup ingredients, and coffee beans—fall from the sky. They were gifts, to be sure, but also hard-earned miracles. Tamar, who shared a room with her mother in the middle room of the *Catholic Worker* offices, became used to her mother giving away one of her two blankets when someone would show up and need a bed to stay warm. How could they keep two when someone else had none? Peter Maurin, who had lived in this manner for many years, approved. Let God expand the walls, he would say, and Dorothy would agree—all the while asking for money, writing articles about the need, and filling her readers in on the daily concerns and experiences of trying to live in solidarity with those who were poor.

As I immersed myself in this time of Dorothy's life, it's hard not to wonder what the world might look like if the bishops and priests had listened to Peter Maurin and Dorothy Day. It's hard not to wonder what the world could look like right now if every-one who could, both then and now, turned a room or a space into a Christ's room. If churches with dwindling numbers converted their buildings into housing for families. If everyone who had a second or third house used it to end the housing crisis. It's hard not to see the parallels between the Great Depression and now, both the issues of the day and also the what ifs. What could happen if we looked to our faith traditions to give us creative solutions to be responsible for each other, especially in times of economic crisis?

The what ifs are personal to me. In Portland, where I live, a person would need to work two full-time minimum-wage jobs to be able to rent a two-bedroom apartment. This statistic is a reality in every major city in the United States (in many cities, it is actually worse).[11] We have accepted this as normal, as our reality under capitalism, but we don't have to. We can reject the current housing market and how it only benefits those who are already in the system. We can work to shelter people from the effects of the greedy, ever-expanding market, and we can work to hopefully change it into something better for everyone. I still dream about this possibility, and Peter and Dorothy make me feel less alone in my desires.

Dorothy knew that her paper went out to thousands of eager Catholics around the country. She was trying to spur on others to pay attention to their own communities—and to prick their conscience to support the *Catholic Worker* by pointing out how dire and immediate the needs were in New York. And it worked—her pieces in the *Catholic Worker* always drummed up the support they needed, right in the nick of time. This became part of the cycle—in trying to meet the overwhelming needs of her neighbors, Dorothy would get in way over her head, be forced to beg for help, and then gleefully celebrate as the "miracles" poured in.

Loaves and fishes, Dorothy knew, came both through prayer and also pounding the pavement. Loaves and fishes, Dorothy knew, were only ordinary items until you found yourself surrounded by a great hungry multitude. Following Jesus meant putting yourself in situations of dire need and then asking for a miracle to save both yourself and your neighbors. Following Jesus meant looking for loaves and fishes wherever you could find them and celebrating when you did.

THE PAPER GROWS, AND SO DOES THE HOUSE

The purpose of a paper is to influence the thought of its readers. We are quite frankly propagandists for Catholic Action. "You may think you are newspaper editors," Father Parsons, the editor of America, *said a few months ago in friendly comment. "But agitators is what you really are."*

—*Catholic Worker* editorial, December 1933

D orothy met with the wildest possible outcome imaginable: her little radical Catholic paper was an overnight success. In the space of just six months, the paper's circulation jumped from 2,500 copies to twenty thousand. Within a year of its first printing, the *Catholic Worker* already surpassed its communist sister paper, the *Daily Worker*, which topped out at thirty-five thousand sub-scriptions. Circulation numbers continued to climb, all the way to a high of over 150,000 subscriptions by May 1938, five years after the *Catholic Worker* started. Given its humble roots and the haphazard ways the paper was often put together, the success was even more surprising. Additional writers and editors were added to the roster, young men and women who were struck by the freshness of the religion being put forth in the *Catholic Worker*. Dorothy was always on the lookout for co-conspirators, assigning people various responsibilities if they stuck around long enough. But as much as she liked to claim otherwise, it was her paper through and through. It was everyone's paper, but it was also distinctly Dorothy's. She fiercely believed in every issue down to every punctuation mark.

The *Catholic Worker* informed its readers of all sorts of intellectual and Catholic thought happening in the United States and Europe. Quotes from various popes were sprinkled throughout, side by side with slice-of-life accounts of what it was like to be a poor washer-woman in New York City. For the Catholic bourgeoisie, it was electrifying, while for the poor workers in New York, it was a paper of solidarity. It spread in part because people passed it out to their friends and neighbors, eager for conversations around the scintillating content. Despite the radical nature of the *Catholic Worker*, more and more parishes and Catholic schools requested subscriptions, causing Dorothy to scramble to print enough issues.

The newspaper was intimately connected to the reality of poverty in New York during the Great Depression. As her audience grew, Dorothy employed her power of words in order to meet the needs of her neighbors. After the first few issues, which dealt exclusively with articles that Dorothy was passionate about—the approach of the paper shifted toward the more personal. Dorothy's chatty columns on life at the *Catholic Worker* offices and the newly expanding houses of hospitality drew readers in. She alternated between a cheerful sort of propaganda highlighting the good and exposés on the dire conditions of poverty as she sought funds to support the paper and the growing work. It was a delicate balance that Dorothy managed to pull off, in part because of her humor and eye for detail. (Eventually, these columns would be titled "On Pilgrimage" and remained a vital draw for new and return subscribers to the paper.)

In 1934, the various apartments and offices coalesced into the first Catholic Worker House, on Charles Street, an eleven-bedroom tenement with women on the third floor, men on the second, and the office and dining room on the first floor. From the beginning, these houses of hospitality were intended as an indictment of the systems of "aid" put forth by the government. Dorothy and Peter were no fans of government welfare and aid because they witnessed how dehumanizing it could be in practice.

Government-sponsored aid programs at that time were not designed to eradicate or even mitigate the suffering of the poor. In many ways, they were designed to punish people for their poverty, to heap misery and shame on those who could not thrive in a capitalistic system. The Catholic Worker Houses, Dorothy decided, would be radically different. Many government or faith-based charity programs like the Salvation Army required people to listen to sermons before they could get their food. Or required addicts and chronic alcoholics to maintain constant sobriety. Dorothy refused these rules—she didn't want to discriminate between who was and who wasn't part of the "worthy" poor. In addition, she wanted to foster a sense of the religious mixed in with art, good literature, and philosophy. She would get artists and muralists to paint the walls, and the clattering of the typewriter for the paper would be a background noise in the midst of the chaos. It would be a place where no one was turned away and where each person was given the dignity of making their own choices on how much to contribute to the cause.

This was all markedly different than any program aimed at helping the poor in New York. And this is because, at heart, Dorothy was an anarchist—she didn't believe in looking to the state for guidance or support, instead looking to the people most impacted by injustice for a way forward. At a young age, she fell in love with the urban masses, and by the time she met Peter Maurin, her love of the common worker became joined with her belief that God made each human as an individual. The world was not made up of the masses, she now believed—it was made up of beloved children of God, each one deserving of dignity and respect and autonomy.

In my cultural framework of modern white evangelicalism, both socialism and anarchism were held up as evils to be avoided at all costs. In Dorothy Day and Peter Maurin, there is a chance for those of us curious about alternate ways of being in the world to have our imaginations sparked. Dorothy's relationship with authority and her own government was confusing, and she was apparently at peace with this.

Her posture toward government authorities was one of extreme suspicion—the "Holy Mother State" is what Dorothy liked to call the government. She disliked much of the conversation surrounding welfare and the New Deal legislation that would start to be enacted shortly after the *Catholic Worker* began. Both she and Peter believed the fate of impoverished people shouldn't be solely in the hands of the state (which had abused, and did abuse, people terribly). They were suspicious of power. They wanted to see a revolution of those who called themselves Christians changing the social order and caring for all of those who suffered. Dorothy and Peter were personalists—they wanted to see average people taking in those who were homeless. They wanted to see a pot of soup and coffee in each kitchen, mutual aid in action. If everyone did their share, if the middle class and the upper class mirrored the hospitality of the poor class, the world would change overnight.

This sounds familiar to what many conservatives have said throughout the years—the responsibility of taking care of poor people should belong to the Church and to the individual. But Dorothy Day defies falling into that camp as well. While she resisted welfare and welfare reforms on an ideological basis, Dorothy and other Catholic workers were quick to sign up their neighbors to receive aid and protections the second they passed and celebrated the minuscule labor victories brought about in the civic square. She wished she didn't live in a world where the government needed to provide housing vouchers for people, but since she did—and they could help families in need—she would sign people up for them.

Her political views in many ways defy the impulse to quickly categorize. She constantly tried to distance herself from communists and had an uneasy relationship with labels like "socialist." But Dorothy had no problem calling herself a Catholic anarchist, referring to herself as one throughout her long life. For her, Christianity, or following Christ, was absolutely connected to anarchism.

Perhaps it is time for more of us who consider ourselves people of faith to engage with the history of Christian anarchism. Jacques Ellul, the French philosopher and well-known Christian anarchist, described his own journey, which echoes aspects of Dorothy's beliefs. He wrote, "The more I studied and the more I understood seriously the biblical message in its entirety . . . the more I came to see how impossible it is to give simple obedience to the state and how there is in the Bible the orientation to a certain anarchism."[1] To follow Jesus meant one could never fully support any nation state, any king, any president. One must only be committed to following Jesus and the values of the kingdom of God.

For Dorothy Day, Peter Maurin, and Jacques Ellul, their anarchism was rooted in the Christian values of nonviolence and neighborly love. Their anarchism was "pacifist, anti-nationalist, anti-capitalist, moral, and antidemocratic anarchism (i.e., that it is hostile to the falsified democracy of bourgeois states)."[2] It was aimed at a true overturning of state authority of all kinds and helping people at the bottom of the manmade hierarchy speak and organize for themselves. Like the beatitudes come to life, they wanted people who had been most disenfranchised in society to be allowed to have the means and power to help themselves and to help others. They wanted to live in a world where the kings were

on the bottom and the peasants were at the top of the social hierarchy. An upside-down kingdom, even in state authority.

This hunger for a world that Jesus spoke of—where the poor
were blessed and those who mourned would find comfort—did
not cause Dorothy to disengage from activity that was distinctly
political in nature. For example, she marched and picketed and
was arrested for the women's suffrage movement—and then never
utilized the right to vote herself. She was arrested, beaten, starved
herself for ten days—and had no desire to engage in what she saw
as a fundamentally flawed system. This is shocking to many but
is completely aligned with Christian anarchist values. Her refusal
to participate in the voting system illuminates the complicated
realities of civic engagement. Even then, Dorothy saw the limitations of voting, for individual states still discriminated against
Black Americans, refusing them the vote until the Voting Rights
Act of 1965. But Dorothy was always up to agitate for those without official power: from the suffragette movement in 1917 and the
struggle of Black Americans in Tennessee as they demanded rights
in 1956 in a state that oppressed them mightily,[3] to the farmwork-
ers union in the 1970s. "Even though the editors of the *Catholic
Worker* do not believe in the vote, in elections as conducted today,
we do agree man wants a part to play, a voice to speak in his community, and this is usually exemplified by the vote,"[4] Dorothy rea-
soned. She, and many others, saw how rigged the system was from
the beginning and did not plan on abdicating the hope of a better
future to politicians alone.

Christian anarchism is not a cheap way to opt out of civic
engagement—on the contrary, Dorothy engaged it in both

profound and surprising ways. She disliked how politics locked one into certain ways of living and being (especially in the two-party system in the United States). To be a person of faith, she learned from Peter Maurin, was to constantly annoy and confuse the people in power and to constantly support those without access to power. The meek would inherit the earth one day, according to Christ. Why not help them scrape out a little bit of it here and now? And if that terrified the people in power, all the better.

The Charles Street Catholic Worker House lasted a little less than a year before it was foreclosed upon by the bank (and it was torn down not much later). The Mott Street house was next, spacious and in a neighborhood rich with Italian immigrants. Mott Street was part of a neighborhood of tenements, small factories, bakeries, stables, laundries, and fish markets. Dorothy began to sprinkle more and more of the everyday life on Mott Street into her writings, and the editorials eventually morphed into a personal, on-the-ground-column that she wrote every month. Household shenanigans and getting in and out of narrow financial scrapes were interspersed with the grim realities of people experiencing poverty and a call for donations to help them keep the work going.

For many subscribers of the paper, reading about those early times at the *Catholic Worker* sounded like a beautiful lark, full of miracles at every turn. When some of them would show up and expect to move into the chaotic and cheerful world Dorothy had written about, they were overwhelmed by the degree to which she and Peter Maurin took seriously living in solidarity with the poor. Christian anarchism, and the hospitality it strove to emulate, was harsh and dreadful in practice indeed.

The Catholic Worker houses were known to be infested with bedbugs. The walls were forever peeling, and personal possessions tended to walk off with sticky-fingered guests. Priests would come for tea and be visibly disturbed by the presence of cockroaches scurrying around. Vermin, pestilence, the smell of unwashed people—it was something that came with the Catholic Worker territory. Many well-meaning people asked Dorothy if it had to be quite so horrid at the Catholic Worker, but she never answered them properly. She resolved to take care of anybody in need and not to place rules on them in order for them to receive hospitality. Nobody was forced to clean or bathe. Nobody was forced to be a temperance advocate (although when use of alcohol turned to violence or in cases of extreme mental instability, the rare intervention was called for). When Dorothy was away on her trips, others would try to implement rules and regulations at the house. On her return, aggrieved guests would complain they were forced to work or perform for their room and board, and Dorothy would sweepingly throw out the rule book.

Dorothy and Peter decided to let God deal with it, and they committed themselves to creating a place where anyone could come, which meant they were committing to helping those who, by all accounts, were very hard people to love. People who did not shower, who did not contribute to the cause in any meaningful way. People who were addicted to substances that could make them loud or violent. Mentally ill people. People who, through no fault of their own, could never make it in society again.

Dorothy did not distinguish between who was or was not "the deserving poor," and in each person, she strove to see the face of Christ. Those working alongside her found this admirable but also wondered, during this intense moment, at the sustainability and wisdom of this mode of operating. I wonder at how unsafe so many must have felt at the Catholic Worker House. And yet Dorothy and Peter insisted that each person was deserving of dignity and respect. In the end, they seemed to draw all the hardest cases to themselves, a frustrating and painful reality that would require Dorothy to invest in a deeply contemplative spiritual practice in order to get through each day.[5]

Dorothy's diaries from this period in her life are full of her private complaints about the types of people God brought the Catholic Worker who tried her patience. Mentally ill women needed her assurance constantly, a listening ear, and a friend to be absorbed in the minute drama of the day. There were men like old Mr. Breen, who had outlived all of his family and was alone, elderly, and a horrific racist. Out of his mouth would spew such vile and racist things even as several other long-term guests loved to antagonize and wind him up. The only person he loved was Dorothy, and he would complain to her bitterly about his fellow neighbors. The Worker had occasional violence to contend with, though less in the early days. The face of poverty slowly shifted; before World War II, most of the people lining up for help and looking for shelter were men of the Bowery, simply looking for work in the Great Depression. In the ensuing decades, the Catholic Worker became a place more and more for the mentally ill and those unable to be a part of the machinations of society. Even in the early years, Dorothy and the Worker were committed to not calling the police and to working with mental health practitioners as much as they could to ensure the safety and dignity of everyone they came into contact with.

Many of these harsher realities Dorothy did not write about publicly, instead striking the cheerful tone of an intrepid adventurer into the colorful world of Mott Street and beyond. Dorothy had a way of making her surroundings come alive in her writings, and it's those rare times when she dips into sadness that I personally find her so compelling. Dorothy had lived in these neighborhoods, surrounded by her poor immigrant neighbors, for long enough to feel the ebb and flow of the community. As she published articles on wage reform and overhauling welfare and how little the United States cared for people in poverty, she also knew how to make it personal.

For her, the harsh winter of 1933 was barreling down the pike, and she missed the smell of fermenting grapes:

If this editorial has a melancholy note, it is not because the chestnuts are wormy or because the stove has cracked, but because all our Italian neighbors are too poor this year to buy grapes and make wine. Grapes that used to be one dollar a box are now one dollar fifty. And the Italian fathers who love their wine and have it in lieu of fresh vegetables and fruits all during the long winter, are still out of jobs or on four-day-month work relief; and this year there is no pleasant smell of fermenting grapes, no disorderly heaps of mash dumped in the gutters.[6]

In many ways, it is easy to see why Dorothy did this: she could write and report about labor issues from a removed distance and advocate for systematic reform. And when it came to issues closer to home—in her own home that she shared with multiple difficult guests—she focused on the good. She trained her eyes to look for beauty where she could, a constant return in her columns and updates. The small pleasures of the poor—homemade wine, religious festivities, cigarettes smoked on the stoop—always impressed themselves upon her. And she grieved with them as what little they had continued to be taken away by a cruel economic system. This grief fueled her to invite others into the sorrows of her neighborhood. She hoped that by pricking the hearts and conscience of others, perhaps things could be better. Perhaps one day, sooner than later, there would be new wine to be drunk with her neighbors.

These times of simple joy were hard-earned. In her journal, Dorothy wrote, "I sit here weeping—I have been torn recently by people, by things that happen. Surely we are, here in our community, made up of poor lost ones, the abandoned ones, the sick, the crazed and the solitary human beings whom Christ so loved and in whom I see, with a terrible anguish, the body of this death."[7] The specialty of the Catholic Worker seemed to be people who were otherwise alone—people who could not, and would never, make it in the landscape of the American dream.

While the New Deal was being enacted in the United States and providing a welcome safety net, Dorothy still saw all the people who were slipping through the cracks, who suffered, alone and unseen. In many ways, it tormented her to think about all of those who must exist in this same state that she could not reach. Her comfort was her faith, her belief in a Christ who knew what it was like to suffer and be lonely. She herself could not reach them all, nor could she convince enough people to take responsibility for their neighbors, try as she might. But at the end of the day, she could trust in a God who saw it all and who, in profound and mysterious ways, was with those who were poor, sick, sad, and lonely.

LOVE IN ACTION

*I am sorry I can say nothing more to console you,
for love in action is a harsh and dreadful thing
compared with love in dreams. Love in dreams is
greedy for immediate action, rapidly performed and
in the sight of all. Men will even give their lives if
only the ordeal does not last long but is soon over,
with all looking on and applauding as though on
stage. But active love is labor and fortitude, and for
some people too, perhaps, a complete science.*

—**Father Zosima** in *The Brothers Karamazov*

Soon after the Catholic Worker office expanded, Peter Maurin began to bring a frequent visitor to the house—Mr. Minas, an immigrant from Armenia (a refugee fleeing war before there was such a legal and political distinction in existence). He had no place to sleep, so both Dorothy and Tamar dutifully offered one of their blankets to him and prepared for him a place to sleep for the night on a cot in the kitchen. From the next morning on, he became a familiar figure, sitting at the kitchen table, drinking coffee with the household, selling the paper in the streets during the day (he was not a good salesperson, thinking more about poetry than the paper). His true focus was on his own project, trying to get statements and pronouncements of various priests and religious folks in Armenia and around the world to condemn fascism. In early 1934, authoritarianism was on the rise in places like Germany and Italy, and there were proponents of fascist thought in the United States as well.

Mr. Minas stayed on as a guest, prompting Dorothy to declare that they were officially an international house. He inserted himself into the daily routine. Dorothy would get up the earliest, go to daily Mass and say her prayers, and then come home and cook breakfast for herself, Tamar, Peter, and Mr. Minas. She would then try to work on the next issue of the paper, answer the large amounts of mail they received daily, and do a small amount of bookkeeping for their haphazard and meager budget. The entire time, Dorothy would receive constant interruptions—between telephone calls and people showing up to talk or requesting help. Nine years old, Tamar roamed the apartment, sometimes playing outside with neighbor friends, sometimes practicing her arithmetic with the Catholic Worker money box (which rarely held much money at all). Mr. Minas, along with a few other devoted souls, would go out into the streets and try to not just sell the paper but convert people to their way of thinking. Another world was possible, the Catholic Church had something to say about the issues of the day—and you, too, could get involved in helping!

While folks were out hawking the paper, other neighbors would drop by and try to persuade Dorothy of the error of her ways. Fascists and anti-Semites were also her neighbors, and Dorothy forced herself to listen to these rants even though she was morally opposed to the ideologies. She was grieved that many Jesuit priests in America were sympathetic to fascism, and she herself had heard some of them "rave against the Jews."[1] An uneasiness was building, even then, in the Catholic Worker house about rumors of wars and what the moral obligation of Catholics was in these times. Dorothy spent time with those regulars who demanded her attention and sympathy, women with both mental and physical needs. She would begin to despair of ever getting all the work done. Of course, she didn't, and then it was time for bed and a new day to start again.

Mr. Minas liked to write poetry in his familiar Armenian script, and he kept it in a small, battered journal on his person at all times. He was amused by Peter Maurin but didn't try to argue or debate with him, preferring to scribble in his journal. Dorothy and Mr. Minas began to have a routine of what she called their "evening repast." After a long day of squabbles, writing, answering urgent questions and needs, cooking food for Tamar and whoever else was around, putting out fires and trying to stoke them in the hearts of her readers, Dorothy and the middle-aged Armenian refugee poet would sit down and quietly share some wine or hot chocolate and bread with mustard or black olives (Mr. Minas liked his with red pepper sprinkled on top). They read Dostoevsky, separate but together—Dorothy choosing *Crime and Punishment*, Mr. Minas choosing *The Idiot*. Dorothy could only find time for reading on the weekends, but she noticed how Mr. Minas carried his copy of *The Idiot* with him wherever he went, always on the lookout for a quiet spot to read—which, she acknowledged, was getting harder and harder to do around the apartment.

He spent his days wandering the streets, mostly alone, sometimes selling a paper or two. Like Tamar, Mr. Minas was drawn more to animals than humans, and there were always a few cats hanging around the Catholic Worker. One black cat they named Social Justice was a favorite of Mr. Minas. He would feed the cat scraps of his own food and pet it constantly. In so many ways, he was a man terribly lost in a new culture, in a time of growing fascism, a political refuge, but he was beginning to find a new home.

One day, Mr. Minas lost his book of poetry. The book was, Dorothy knew, a treasure beyond comprehension for the poor man. He had no possessions to his name; nothing of his family or culture or past had been brought with him to America. He had only the poems he slowly wrote and copied down, inscrutable to all except himself and God. And now they had vanished.

Search parties were organized; people looked in Union Square and all the haunts where he would have gone out to sell the paper. With the loss, the mood around the house was somber. Together, the house prayed and prayed and prayed.

And then—a miracle occurred. A small boy knocked on their door the following day, holding the journal of poetry. The address had been written on the inside cover. One of the women who was a regular at the Worker exclaimed immediately that the boy at the door was St. Anthony himself, patron saint of lost things ("Oh no," said the little boy, "I'm Episcopalian"). There was so much joy and celebration in the house that day when the pearl of great price was found, the poetry that no one but Mr. Minas could read. Social Justice the cat got an extra tidbit of cheese that night, and from that point on, Mr. Minas always safety-pinned the journal to the inside of his coat pocket.

Dorothy recorded the incident in her journal because the miracles and celebrations and evening rituals of bread with mustard were all so important to her. She saw in Mr. Minas and his poetry the kind of people Jesus was drawn to, like the widow who lost her coin. She knew that for all the troubles and strife they experienced, the community forming around the Catholic Worker—the cats and the kids and the poets with no place to lay their head—they were also learning how to celebrate the miracles where they could find them.[2]

A small but growing cast of characters like Mr. Minas attached themselves to Dorothy and the Worker, some of them staying with her until the day they died. In her books, she describes these people tenderly, with an eye for the good in them—though that didn't mean they were easy roommates or comrades to share life with. There were folks like Dorothy Weston, a young Irish woman who came on to help Dorothy as an editor of the paper, bringing with her a scholar's heart for understanding the issues of the day. Or people like Stanley Vishnewski, a seventeen-year-old Lithuanian boy who started helping out by selling the paper and running errands and then kept deciding to help out until he died in 1979. He was a voice of working-class faith and charming good humor at the Catholic Worker for decades and never failed to humanize Dorothy for those who were intimidated by her. "Once you get to know her, she's just another crabby old lady!"[3] he would assure them.

There was "Big Dan," who joined the crew early and who was huge and loud and brash and asked that he might have a basin of warm water to soak his feet the first night he came in. An unemployed man, he slept on the piers and ate food out of garbage cans, wearing shoes too small for his feet, toes poking out of holes. Peter noticed this and made preparations to wash his feet. As he did so, Peter began indoctrinating Big Dan, as he would do with anyone sitting in front of him. Dorothy watched the two of them, fascinated—Peter yelling, "Fire the bosses," Big Dan enthusiastically egging him on. Dorothy noticed how Big Dan sat up a little straighter, eyes sparkling. Dorothy knew that he didn't understand the intricacies of Peter's ideologies, but he could easily catch on to the idea that no boss would know how to live his life. In real time, Dorothy saw people catch a spark that had all but been extinguished on the streets—the reality that they could be proud to be poor and to dream of a life not under the thumb of a harsh and uncaring economic system.[4]

Almost immediately, Big Dan became a part of the Catholic Worker, starting with selling the papers out on the streets. With his tall stature and big booming voice, he quickly became one of their best sellers (he loved to shout over the communists trying to sell the *Daily Worker*). All of this, combined with his gigantic smile, made Dorothy say he was the best public-relations man they ever could have hired. Big Dan wasn't afraid to leave the neighborhood and sometimes went all the way uptown to the fancy Macy's store and hawked his radical Catholic paper for a penny a copy there (it's unclear how many people snapped up that offer on Fifth Avenue). Dorothy said that passing out copies of the *Catholic Worker* makes one look like the fool but that Christ promised that the foolish things of the world would shame the wise.[5] To Dorothy, Big Dan in front of Macy's shouting at people to come and join the revolution was a picture of this great, foolish mystery.

The immediate success of the paper with Catholics and with intellectuals of the day went a little bit to their heads, Dorothy later said. Although many priests and bishops were inundated with concerns about the anarchist nature of the paper, so, too, did the reports fly in of people all across the country—and indeed the world—being inspired by it. Some of the best minds of the day wanted to read the paper, write for the paper, and have their ideas discussed in the paper. In the first few months in the swirl of people coming by for soup and bread and hours of talking, distinguished guests started to show up. Dorothy declared that the best was none too good for the poor, so she invited the most prominent priests of the time to visit, and prominent French philosophers and writers were known to show up as well, including the likes of Jacques Maritain and Hilaire Belloc.

It could be an interesting juxtaposition at times. One time, Stanley was there, eating his dinner in the kitchen. Margaret, the cook, was busy with the soup and bread of the day. Mary Sheenan, the young Irish woman who came every day to the Catholic Worker to hang out and sell papers, was also there eating with Big Dan and Dorothy as some of the Big Important Men were talking outside to a group of rapt listeners. Big Dan remarked with awe in his voice, "If we paid these men for their lectures, they would get one hundred dollars apiece." Mary Sheenan was less impressed. Pouring herself another cup of coffee, she snapped back, "If they're so great, why don't you sit in there and listen to them?"[6]

Peter loved that these distinguished thinkers and gentlemen found their way to the Catholic Worker house and delighted in the long discussions happening into the wee hours of the night. He read some of the letters flowing in praising the paper and the ideas discussed therein, and Dorothy noted that he began to get some stars in his eyes. He went out one day and rented a large ballroom to host his own "clarification of thought meeting" (with himself as the star speaker) and advertised it around town. This was a leap too big for the organic, messy, anarchist nature of the discussions happening at the Catholic Worker offices, and on the fateful day of Peter's big event, only fifteen people showed up to that large, cavernous ballroom. Peter did not complain about the turnout but never again rented a ballroom for such events.

Another notable guest from this time period was Ade Bethune. A teenage immigrant from Belgium to New York City, Ade was young, artistically minded, and curious about the world. She read the first few issues of the *Catholic Worker* and thought it could use some illustrations since it was mostly intense print crammed together with little else. Ade liked the visual style of the communist tabloids she had seen floating around and tried her hand at illustrating a few saints including St. Joseph, the man Catholic Workers were most likely to appeal to for funds to keep their work going. She later said that she didn't understand much about the unions and labor issues, but she understood the hospitality part of the paper. Ade was also interested in the works of mercy and in highlighting the saints of old fulfilling these practical acts of hospitality—feeding and clothing and visiting those sick and imprisoned—and doing it in modern-style dress. We all could be like the saints, she believed, doing the practical work of love.

Ade sent off a sample of her illustrations to the *Catholic Worker* with a letter that said, "There is but one thing I can make: that is pictures." When she showed up the next month with two bags full of clothes to donate and to get a glimpse of the place, Dorothy Day thought she had no home and was looking for a place to sleep. No, Ade stammered out, painfully shy. "I'm the girl who made the pictures for you." "Oh," said Dorothy, surprised. Then she sat down and gave Ade all the illustration ideas she would like for future editions, with some notes on how to best portray the saints of each month. This was how Ade became the visual artist for the paper, how her liturgical works inspired people around the globe.

At first, Ade was overwhelmed by Dorothy—describing her as a woman with a face carved by an ax, with wide eyes on either side of her face like a doe, full of kindness but also wit and sarcasm. In contrast, she immediately warmed to Peter Maurin—she was charmed by his gentle demeanor and his Easy Essays and his glasses held together by paper clips. And while both he and Dorothy mentored Ade, it was Peter who constantly pushed her past her shyness and encouraged her to speak and even got her to hawk the newspaper occasionally.

Like Dorothy, Ade Bethune became a shining pupil under Peter's tutelage, although both women possessed greatly different temperaments and giftings. Ade held her artistry with the same amount of love and care that Peter wished everyone would approach their craft with—be it farming, woodworking, machine working, mothering, or art. Ade infused her work with love and a desire to bring communities together. In the beginning, Dorothy received some complaints about Ade's images from fellow activist-minded people: the illustrations were too cheerful, not grim or angry enough for the state of the world. But Dorothy loved them. She told Ade she wanted beautiful things in her paper—"vineyards, people working in gardens, children," all good things. The world was bad enough, and they didn't need to add to it. To this day, it is the artistry and style of Ade that infuse the *Catholic Worker*, centering the articles and updates with beauty, history, and goodness. The liturgical nature of her designs asks viewers to rest their eyes on familiar images of saints and parable scenes but consider them afresh.

Stanley, Mr. Minas, Peter, Tamar, Mary Sheenan, Big Dan, Ade Bethune—in the early years, these were among the crew of people from all walks of life who joined Dorothy. Now the woman who always felt lonely in her longing for God and a better world couldn't find a moment of solitude and peace. As the houses grew, so did the noise, the squalor, and the conflict. "A house of hostility," Stanley would walk around muttering.[7] The Catholic Worker faced many criticisms both from the outside world and from those who came to be part of it. After a while, those who came to stay would wonder about alternative ways of doing things. But for the most part, it was Dorothy's way or the highway—which is how jokes emerged about her being an anarchist except when it came to challenging her beliefs and ideas.[8]

These stories of the beginnings of the Catholic Worker are full of humor and failure and grassroots camaraderie and heady days. As the movement grew, people began to explore the idea of starting houses of hospitality themselves around the country, each one having its own distinct feel. Dorothy recognized with a thrill that it wasn't just her and Peter and the crew, after all. There was a hunger, a palpable need, for people to understand that the Catholic Church had a plan of social action to change the world for the better, right here and right now—and that all were invited to be a part of it: professors, workers, refugees, old people, infirm individuals, the jovial and crabby. Love in action could be a harsh and dreadful thing, but it was certainly never, ever boring.

PART 3

THE WORK
CONTINUES

THE DUTY OF DELIGHT

My mother used to say, "When you are in the dumps, clean house, take a bath, dress up, go downtown and window-shop." Everything passes, St. Teresa of Avila says.

—**Dorothy Day** in her diary, June 18, 1970

The diaries of Dorothy Day are their own nervous system of tunneling roots, fragmentations, and scattered, delightful moments—full of names and dates and places, a record of her travels and her desire to be a better neighbor to the people she lived with and who got on her nerves constantly. And near the end of her life, her mind wandering a bit, her stories and books and poems and musical influences bloomed at different times in her memory. When the diary entries slowed to a trickle, after a small heart attack confined her to bed much of the time, she often had a Dostoevsky quote she returned to: "The world will be saved by beauty." Time and again, she wrote it down, even as her own vine was withering.[1]

When I've heard others quote Dostoevsky's line or see it in curly font on a bright mug, it makes me angry. *The world will be saved by beauty.* Tell this to people who are working three jobs to pay the rent, who have applied for family members to immigrate to the United States but were just informed the program has been shut down; tell this to people in the grips of addiction and disease and despair; tell this to the kid who goes to school hungry every morning. Try telling people who are in immense suffering that beauty will save the world, in your smooth voice and with an untroubled face, and see how that goes for you.

But when Dorothy quotes Dostoevsky, she had suffering in mind—when she quotes him, she is thinking about his entire collection of works, his oeuvre, his entire philosophy of the world. When, in 1973, she was reflecting on forty years of the Catholic Worker movement, she said, "I do not think I could have carried on with a loving heart all these years without Dostoyevsky's understanding of poverty, suffering, and drunkenness." When she quoted Dostoevsky at the end of her life, she understood his thick novels crammed full of terrible and funny and sad moments—and those that reflected the lives of the mentally ill. The pages and pages and pages spent on lament, on calling out the world for just how bad it was and just how messed up humans could be, when—out of nowhere—beauty would show its face and change everything. Father Zosima's perfume smell, the story of the onion, a moment of kindness shared with a peasant, a meal gorgeously rendered into print. Bright bursts of beauty meant more to people like Dostoevsky and Dorothy Day because they knew how hard-earned it was. For them, beauty was a sign of the resilience of humanity in the face of cruelty. A sign of resurrection. A small redemption of all the misery the earth endured. And it pointed to a God who was present and good, despite all evidence to the contrary. It reminded Dorothy that God was a creator, delighting in creation of all types. A sweet strawberry, a good cup of coffee, a freshly rolled cigarette, a beautiful piano piece, a play put on by one of her friends, a Russian novel. Each one a precious gift to be savored, to give strength to the one who needs to get up and face the realities of the world again and again.

In her diaries, Dorothy also wrote about what she called "the duty of delight." Making the conscious decision to meditate on the good things the world has to offer as a spiritual practice, a discipline of sorts. The duty of delight was a way for Dorothy to acknowledge and engage in the totality of a sinful, systematically unequal and unjust world and still find ways to be met with what Dostoevsky called beauty, what others call grace. At the end of her life, there in her cramped little room with a shelf full of beloved Russian novels, Dorothy dreamed of this phrase—"the world will be saved by beauty." She did not dream about writing one more screed about labor unions, or racism, or militarism, or capitalism. She wanted to dream about beauty.

And that means something to me.

Sometimes I joke that I am very good at practicing the duty of despair. The opposite of the duty of delight, it often feels like my eyes are trained to see all the bad in the world. I see suffering, I see inequality, I see how connected I am to systems that oppress and marginalize—and I don't see how I can rest, or be happy, or experience joy when not everyone in the world is flourishing.

There are seeds of the savior complex in my own temperament: I often become weighed down by the desire to fix complex and centuries-old issues with my own two hands. My despair doesn't actually help anyone or make the world a better place for my neighbors. So I paid close attention to all the times Dorothy wrote about her simple life pleasures and the duty of delight. I paid close attention, because I know how much help I need to be able to move forward in a world that is both filled with joy and filled with injustice.

While researching and writing this book, the world was set on fire. I signed my book contract in March of 2020, when COVID-19 first shut down our schools, churches, and neighborhood gatherings. My neighbors scrambled for food, to pay the rent after being laid off. My children struggled in isolation. Black Lives Matter protests broke out that first summer in response to the murder of George Floyd. I joined the protests in Portland and was tear-gassed repeatedly by federal police officers for simply holding a sign that said "Mother Mary knows what it is like to lose a son to state violence."

Wildfires raged across Oregon, a symptom of the pressing reality of climate change. The sun glowed an eerie orange color while we were trapped inside our houses for a week at a time, unable to safely breathe the ash-laden air. White evangelicals, my people, were making the news for protesting mask mandates and for refusing to follow public health guidelines to minimize the spread of a deadly virus. A caustic and polarizing presidential election ensued, with the majority of my community voting for Donald Trump and refusing to acknowledge the election of Joe Biden. Political instability in countries like Myanmar and Afghanistan impacted me personally as I had so many friends and neighbors anxious about loved ones who couldn't escape to safety.

Mental health crises soared, both in general and in my own family. I continued to homeschool my children, processing my own grief at how quickly my life had turned upside down. Was this the new normal? Trapped at home, my own anxiety skyrocketing, reading headline after headline about overcrowded hospitals and police violence and Christians advocating for a rush back to normal, no matter how many people died?

I struggled. Reading about Dorothy Day and the Catholic Worker, I missed my own old life—the English classes, the walks to school, the rhythms of being a neighbor and friend. A deadly pandemic that made it unsafe to be around people was my worst nightmare, and here I was being forced to live through it. People I knew died of COVID-19, alone and in a hospital, convinced vaccines wouldn't help. The duty of despair threatened to overwhelm me. But how can one find delight during such unprecedented times? I didn't know the answer to this, but reading Dorothy's words compelled me to keep my eyes wide open in case something good could be born in the midst of great upheaval.

I thought about the duty of delight the other day when my good friend and neighbor came over. Together, she and I had spent months trying to figure out ways to advocate for her family members to get out of Afghanistan. Nothing we did worked. I had lost hope in all the bureaucracies of my country; I knew that fundamentally we were an unwelcoming place with immigration policies that did not prioritize at-risk people. But once again, we were going to go through the stacks of paperwork and try to get multiple relatives on the radar of the US government.

My friend was sad; I could see it in her eyes, her face. Her shoulder ached at night so that she couldn't sleep. She couldn't bake bread anymore or even sew. She was collecting cans to send money to relatives—if you don't help your family out right now, she told me, then they will no longer be your family. Her phone was constantly buzzing—desperate requests from various people asking for money, help, aid, and for a path for them to be able to come and live in safety. The Taliban had taken over Kabul, and people were scared. Jobs were scarce, winter was setting in, and there wasn't enough food.

"My niece called me today," my friend told me. "She called because she had a dream about me." This niece is married to a man who was an interpreter for the US Army for many years, who by all accounts should have been resettled in the United States but was left behind for the Taliban to target. They are trapped in their country, considered enemies now by the people who are in power. No matter how many forms we filled out, there was never any news. No one ever contacted them. They lived their lives waiting, waiting, waiting.

"What was the dream?" I asked. "She dreamed that she and I were together, that we were walking together in the snow. We were talking, visiting, and walking as the snow fell down, slowly, slowly." My friend told me this, and both of us were quiet for a very long time. My eyes filled with tears as I envisioned this scene.

The stillness of a snowy day, the loveliness of visiting with a family member you have not seen in years. My friend looked at me, and she also was teary. "Maybe there is hope," she said. "Maybe one day we will walk together in the beautiful snow."

I think about the dream, the snow, the hope that seems almost too precious to hold. And I think this is what the duty of delight truly is: the ability to see the world and all of its terrors while still holding on to hope.

Grief permeates our world. Like the events of the 1930s, we are at another turning point. The bread lines are long, rents are rising, livable wages are hard to find. But in the shadow of great turmoil, hope arises. In times of great suffering, so, too, do we see humanity—especially at the margins—rise up and declare another way is possible. We do not need to accept this world as it is. We can point out how flawed it is, how much it hurts us and others, and we can do something to change it.

Another world is possible. It is right around the corner; I can almost feel it with my fingertips. A world where everyone is treated as a beloved child of God. A world where those who have survived the worst life has to offer are given a space to finally rest. A snowy walk with loved ones, the muffled sounds of laughter and tears. A world, broken seemingly beyond repair, stitched together with delight.

It's my duty to pay attention to the suffering. And it is my duty to pay attention to delight. Dorothy Day taught me this, along with all of my neighbors who have survived the ends of their own worlds. Together, we hope; together, we delight. Together, we live another day, connected to each other.

JUST SITTING AROUND TALKING

*We were just sitting there talking when
lines of people began to form, saying,
"We need bread."*

We could not say, "Go, be thou filled."

*If there were six small loaves and a few fishes, we had to
divide them.*

There was always bread.

*We were just sitting there talking and people moved in on
us.*

Let those who can take it, take it.

Some moved out and that made room for more.

And somehow the walls expanded.

—From the Epilogue of *The Long Loneliness*

Dorothy wrote a famous postscript to *The Long Loneliness* that reads like a poem, as though it happened as organically as a long and somewhat haphazard dinner party: "We were sitting around talking when Peter Maurin came in. We were sitting around talking when lines of people began to form, saying 'we need bread.' . . . We were just sitting around talking and people moved in on us. . . . We were just sitting around talking when someone said 'let's all go live on a farm.' . . . It was as casual as all that, I often think. It just came about. It just happened."

Her postscript, similar in some ways to the Easy Essays of Peter Maurin, makes it all seem like a fever dream that happened to someone else. The work of putting out a paper, constantly speaking at Catholic churches, renting multiple apartments and filling them with people who had nowhere else to go. The countless meals served and conversations had, the constant struggle to pay bills and meet the needs of those showing up at the door, the hours of prayer and daily Mass, dealing with intellectuals dropping by for a visit and a fellow roommate in the depths of a mental health crisis—it all just seemingly happened. The farms, the mortgages, the constant retreats. The paper being written, edited, and published every month. The squabbles within the community, the tensions with the Catholic hierarchy, the constant picketing and protests and soup lines and coffee pots: "Let those who can take it, take it. Some people moved out and made room for more. Somehow, the walls expanded."

In that one little word *somehow*, there is a lot left out. Or maybe that word just contains multitudes, the story of her life stripped down to the bare essentials, loaves and fishes, soup and coffee, we were just sitting around talking, and it continues on to this day.

"Dorothy lives on a bus," Stanley Vishnewski would say. "She started the Catholic Worker and the rest of us have to live in it."[1] As much as the Catholic Worker house depended on Dorothy to run it, she was always escaping her communal life. Oftentimes, the bus rides crisscrossing the country were the only times she was alone, and she relished the chance to journal and reflect. Dorothy accepted nearly every invitation she got to speak in those early years. She roamed the country on a bus or in old shoddy cars and covered strikes and labor issues and spoke about the Catholic Worker house and did everything possible to grow the movement. She found herself in the delicate balance of both leading the movement at home and needing to travel in order to further the cause. And there was also her own drive and curiosity to contend with.

In 1936 alone, Dorothy traveled and reported on a variety of important strikes in the United States: she went to Detroit for the automobile workers; Massachusetts for textile workers; Pittsburgh for steel; Akron, Ohio, for rubber; and the Gulf Coast for shrimp. She ended the year in New York, where she and the Catholic Worker community supported the seamen's strike so enthusiastically that partially due to their support, the National Maritime Union was established.

At that time, so many maritime workers were on strike and milling about the city that the Catholic Worker, at significant financial cost, set up in the west side of the city and operated a soup and bread line just to support those workers longing for more rights. They fed thousands of men a day, peanut butter and cottage cheese and jam and bread and coffee, going into debt just to keep the endeavor running (Dorothy noted disapprovingly that people loved to donate to charity but drew the line at supporting striking workers, which they found too similar to communism). For three months, the second bread line helped the striking seamen keep their resolve, until eventually a negotiation was reached.[2]

But Dorothy wasn't just reporting on strikes for her newspaper. Whatever town she was in, she would also connect with the local Catholic churches and parish schools. She spoke wherever she could get a toe in, and despite not being an incredibly skilled orator, she inspired people—especially the young—wherever she went. For all the public speaking she did, Dorothy always claimed to hate it. Was it nerves? Was it her quick mind, always struggling to know what to say to move the audience in the direction she wanted? She was certainly aware of all the pushback she faced on multiple sides. If more houses of hospitality were to spring up, Dorothy needed to be crossing the country, looking for like-minded workers. The Catholic Worker also needed money. It didn't receive official financial support from the Catholic Church, and it received no government aid. In many ways, it was left to Dorothy, and the twice-a-year pleas they put out in the newspaper, and her constant traveling to bring in the money to fund the work.

Dorothy was aware of the power she held in the Catholic Worker community and from early on recognized her role as the face of the movement. People depended on her to implement the practicalities but also for inspiration. It was a heavy burden to bear. When she was home, a delightful and exasperating chaos was her new normal. And as much as she pleaded for anarchistic ideals, Dorothy was very much in a hierarchical structure: she was the one in charge. People knew and respected Peter Maurin for his ideas and his incredible religious education, but he wasn't the person you went to when you needed to solve a problem. When you had a problem, you went to Dorothy Day. She often joked about being in the horrible position of a dictator constantly looking to legislate herself out of a job. In her diaries, she wrote how if she was discouraged, then everyone around her would fall into the depths of despair and "hopeless anger." But if she was not discouraged, then those around her would try to make her see how bad the world was and become angry with her placid good cheer.

She must, Dorothy thought, try and become more like Peter Maurin and be oblivious to the emotional needs and desires of those around her, for she was always sure to disappoint someone. Especially those higher-ups who read her paper every month with increasing nervousness. Just what, oh what, was that blasted *Catholic Worker* paper going to say next?

Tension with the hierarchy of the Catholic Church was a constant theme in Dorothy's life but one she could not talk about easily, partially because it was so intensely personal. Throughout her entire life, she struggled to reconcile her love of God and the life Jesus called her to with the hypocrisies of the Church she had promised herself to. But she was also aware of the dangers of self-righteousness within herself and other people banging the drum for social and moral reform and tried to keep a sense of humor even in the midst of her reforming personality.

Once, a priest came to one of her and Peter's roundtable discussion nights and decided to lecture the crowd on how spirituality was of utmost importance and they must not focus too much on earthly things like economics. Dorothy shot out of her chair and said, "You can't preach the gospel to men with empty stomachs!" and proceeded to ask the priest if he had even been to the municipal lodging house and seen the seventeen thousand men gathered for meals and a bed. Because if you *had*, said Dorothy, then surely you would see that it is necessary to put some emphasis on material conditions when we preach the good news.[3]

The paper itself made many lay Catholics and priests alike nervous. Priests like Father Gratry would visit the office just to tell Dorothy that "reading newspapers is a waste of time" because "one loses sight of the eternal." Or there was Father Corbett, who dropped in to tell her that "people say that you do too much criticizing and don't point out all that is being done." Good Catholics were annoyed that Dorothy did not highlight the positives of the Church enough. To that, Dorothy wrote in her December 1933 issue, "We agree that much is being done—but so much more remains. 'Never rest, never rest, there's no peace on earth,' we say cheerfully with our patron saint Teresa of Avila."[4]

Angry readers regularly called on priests to condemn Dorothy's or the paper's positions. But since Dorothy was a layperson, the priests had very little jurisdiction over her. While many were pained that "Catholic" was part of her newspaper title, there was little to be done about it. Dorothy used her lack of power and privilege in the Church to great advantage, painting an air of being blissfully unaware of conflict with the diocese until she was called upon to answer for the paper (which she did, taking full responsibility for the contents put forth). Still, Dorothy did eventually make some concessions, including bringing on a like-minded priest to be an advisor to the paper.

There is something beautiful in the defiant way Dorothy interacted with the Catholic Church, especially those in positions of power. She wanted so badly for the Church to live up to its stated ideals. As the years crept toward America's involvement in World War II, she found herself in the unique position of elevating and putting forth elements of the Catholic faith and history into the public consciousness while also clashing publicly with the same religious tradition. She quoted the papal encyclicals and went to Mass daily and encouraged people to do the same—she wished that all who joined the Catholic Worker would convert to Catholicism and was disappointed when they didn't. At the exact same time, she had no problem pointing out the hypocrisies in the faith of mayors and police officers and even the archbishop of New York (whom she went head to head with multiple times).

As with many other people throughout the years, her Catholicism only made sense to her in the context of the Catholic Worker community, when it was lived out in voluntary poverty and in giving and receiving the works of mercy.[5] While many others—including her daughter and most of her grandchildren—left the faith, Dorothy never did. She also never left the Worker, stubbornly remaining in solidarity with the poor and stubbornly committed to her chosen religion. She was a thorn in the side of the Catholic

Church, and she was also one of their most devout lay leaders. Her eyes would sparkle as people tried to figure her out. *Let them take their time,* I imagine her thinking. She liked confusing people; she liked slipping through the cracks. But more than anything, she liked getting the work done.

I n 1952, Dwight McDonald wrote a *New Yorker* profile of Dorothy Day so extensive that it ended up requiring two issues. He wrote that one of the reasons the *Catholic Worker* was so successful in the 1930s—why it reached circulation rates of around 150 thousand, why so many Catholics seemed eager for a way to get involved with the plight of the poor in their country, why houses of hospitality and places where people would gather to discuss these ideas mushroomed across the country—was because of the direct action approach Dorothy Day espoused, coupled with the absolute rock bottom of the Depression for people in need. It was a perfect storm, a spontaneous combustion of need and someone with an answer to the overwhelming problems facing the country.[6]

The folks who gathered at the Catholic Worker weren't just sitting around talking, as it turns out. They were people obsessed with simple, direct actions—soup for the hungry, coffee for the tired and thirsty, jackets for the cold, apartments for those who were homeless. They didn't wait around for committees and hierarchies and approval and funds. Dorothy Day and Peter Maurin just went out and did things—starting a soup kitchen or picketing for the rights of workers or renting yet another tenement building to house more people. The walls didn't just miraculously grow to expand. Dorothy Day went out and rented buildings, lived in them, wrote about them, traveled around the country to talk about them, and then came back and did it all over again, with an increasingly larger crowd of like-minded people joining her constantly.

When the printers would call for the bill, when the grocer and the butcher needed to be paid, when the electricity and the mortgages of several houses and farms were pressing on Dorothy's shoulders alone, she would always assure anyone listening that St. Joseph—the patron saint of those in dire need of help, and thus of the Catholic Worker—would take care of it. They wore out the saint's ears with their constant prayers. When it came time to pay, the printers would ask, "Who is this Joseph person, and why does he consent to pay at the very last second?"

In her writing, advocacy, and continuous interactions with the Catholic priests and bishops who asked about her work, she insisted that it was the everyday people who were called on to provide for each other. Instead of only appealing to saints, we were to actually start to live like them. Dorothy was trying to make a case for the beauty of a life lived in mutual aid—when you hear of a neighbor in need, you try to fulfill it, trusting that when our turn came to ask for another blanket, some other St. Joseph in disguise would be there to give it to us. Somewhere, somehow, someone had an empty room or apartment. Someone had vegetables to throw in the soup. Someone had a blanket or coat to donate, taking up all that space in their closet instead of warming up Christ himself on the streets. Someone, surely, had extra loaves and fishes lying around for the hordes of hungry people in their city. But if you were never in need, if you never had to ask for yourself or for a friend, how could you ever be blessed by the miracles Christ himself performed?

Perhaps that is the mystery she explores in her postscript: "We cannot love God unless we love each other, and to love we must know each other. . . . We have all known the long loneliness and we have learned that the only solution is love and that love comes with community. It all happened while we sat there talking, and it is still going on."[7]

At first I felt frustrated by how much Dorothy left out in her epilogue to *The Long Loneliness*, how easy and organic she made it seem. I am living through a time where the needs of my community are so great, and I don't know what to do next. But perhaps that was the point; perhaps she was also making room for people to live out their own stories of the movement. To see themselves invited into the adventure and love and work of the long loneliness, the call to try to love your neighbor as yourself. To see themselves caught up in a movement bigger than themselves. And even now, she is inviting us to consider a life lived in a way where we can and must depend on our neighbors to see a better world come to fruition. It could happen to us even now. While we are sitting here talking, reading, thinking. It is all happening, right outside our doors, if only we have the eyes to see it.

MOTHER OF A
MOVEMENT

*To have known Dorothy means spending the rest of
your life wondering what hit you.*

—**Kate Hennessey**, granddaughter of Dorothy Day

A resident of Mott Street who was six when she first met Dorothy Day remembered her clearly: "When I first saw her, I thought she was a foreigner, you know, because she was dressed in dark colors, except for a white blouse and a kerchief around her head. . . . She stuck out like a sore thumb, she really did. She looked like somebody just off the boat. She was tall, with no makeup and stunning eyes. Beautiful! As far as I was concerned, the woman was a saint because she'd be at mass every day and always walking around with her prayer missal but dressed like a peasant."[1] The neighbors on Mott Street were curious about the tall, plainly dressed woman who brought a ragtag group of people with her to live in the large house and who soon had hundreds of men lining up for coffee and bread every single morning. To Dorothy's relief, no one complained as they watched the gathering destitute groups form in their neighborhood, the lines snaking down the block. They watched Dorothy walk to Mass every day, the picture of a devout Catholic woman. She was pious, poor, and drew the oppressed to her wherever she was. People began to whisper among themselves, wondering if this woman was a saint. If this suggestion was ever brought up to Dorothy, she would snap at anyone who suggested such a ridiculous thing. "Bullshit," she would say and get back to her work.[2]

As the destitute groups gathered on Mott Street, she was still integrating all the parts of herself: her activism, her journalistic eye, her ambition. Yes, she wore plain dresses and stopped getting her hair cut into stylish bobs (she didn't like the expense or upkeep of short haircuts). Her hair began to grow longer and grayer, and eventually she took to putting it into her signature braids, which she wrapped around her head. But in the 1930s, she was a striking-looking woman, described as beautiful, handsome, and stunning by men and women alike. Her face at times looked passive, except for her mouth, which refused to behave and could quirk into a smile or a frown. She wore French berets and little fedoras, smoked constantly (and rolled her own cigarettes), and struggled not to swear every time she was angry or annoyed.

She was still a bundle of contradictions, a woman who just a few years ago longed to be at the center of the New York literary scene with her novels and plays. And now here she was, the mother of many wayward sons and daughters, the matron of the Catholic Worker community. She wanted to live like a saint but not be treated like a plaster statue of one. She never could fit inside the mold anyway, and early on she stopped trying.

I wonder when Dorothy Day realized she had inadvertently become the mother of a movement of radical Catholic teaching and direct action. Dorothy found herself not just in the thick of it but the uneasy leader of it all. She was the unofficial house mom for multiple apartments of people (all of whom had experienced various levels of trauma and systematic oppression). She oversaw to some degree the coffee, bread, and soup lines that the Worker maintained every day. She wrote and edited the majority of the monthly paper, many of the pieces requiring journalistic reporting. She was the main person to read and respond to correspondence from readers and to entertain visitors, and she was the one called upon to give answers whenever the Catholic Church became overly uneasy about one of the positions stated in her paper. She felt the weight of requesting funds to keep the fast-growing work going. It was exciting work but exhausting all the same. And underneath it all ran the constant worry that she wasn't doing right by her daughter. She worried, like so many women do, if she could keep all the plates spinning. She worried, all the time, if she was being a bad mother.

Dorothy Day was still a mother to a young child when this new movement was being birthed. Tamar was seven when she helped her mother pass out the first issue of the *Catholic Worker* in Union Square. She was always around during those first days as people started to move into the Mott Street building, as downstairs became the Catholic Worker offices and the kitchen. Dorothy and Tamar were a package deal, and Tamar was plunged into life at the Worker whether she liked it or not.

Tamar grew into a private person who was fiercely protective of her mother's legacy. When she talked about growing up in the Catholic Worker house, she mostly emphasized the positives: how so many people helped raise her, the sense of community and adventure she experienced there. She loved to be near her mother and Peter Maurin when they were holding court in a room packed full of people eager to change the world (though perhaps, Tamar mused, the chain smoking going on wasn't the best for her young lungs).

"They were all such wonderful fools, so full of hope," Tamar reflected. "Those early years were magnificent. . . . So many people came in off the streets and blossomed at the Worker." As her world was shaped by her surroundings, Tamar thought this is how every-one lived their life, that the world was fundamentally full of kind and good people who would always take care of the broken and damaged among them, that hospitality and radical welcome were the norm.[3] As she grew older, she was saddened to realize this was not the way the world worked, even as she valued even more the love modeled at the Worker.

Tamar was the only child consistently living at the Catholic Worker house, and Dorothy was quick to write about the bless-ings of this—Tamar did not have just one mother but so many aunties and uncles who looked out for her.[4] Tamar met people and characters who would remain in her life for decades whom she loved completely. There was Peter Maurin, of course, and Stanley

Vishnewski. Joe and Gerry were a part of the Worker, and together with young Tamar, they formed what they called the Hot Chocolate Club. If Tamar came home for a weekend or school break and her mother was out traveling, the Hot Chocolate Club would take long walks around the city, visiting museums and parks, always stopping to get a cup of hot chocolate.

But despite all the emphasis on the positives, for a shy child deeply attached to her mother, life at the Worker could be hard, scary, and lonely. A former Catholic Worker remarked that Dorothy was a classic founder—think Steve Jobs or Bill Gate—and, as such, Tamar experienced the tragedy of being a founder's child: sometimes neglected in favor of the enormity of "the work." Tamar nicknamed Dorothy "Be-going" during this time as her mother was always leaving to travel and drum up support for the work. "I wanted Dorothy so bad," she later reminisced about those early years. And "when she came home she lit up my room, she lit up my whole life,"[5] Tamar said.

At a young age, Tamar was already being saddled with expectations that she would grow up to be like her mother, but she knew early on that she took after her father more. Beyond just being shy, many remarked that she was odd and lacked social skills such as looking people in the eye when she talked to them. Her daughter, Kate Hennessy, has disclosed that later in life, Tamar wondered if she might be somewhere on the autism spectrum.[6] Tamar was drawn to nature, to animals, and to retreating from the world at times. It's easy to envision how such a temperament was often at odds with the frenetic pace of the Worker. Tamar made friends with neighbor children and took care of stray animals and played in the tiny garden. When she was home, she slept in the same room as Dorothy and became used to giving away her possessions (or sometimes having them stolen by jealous or mentally ill guests).

Dorothy was locked into the whirlwind of keeping her paper and houses of hospitality afloat. The urgency of the moment in labor issues and the explosion of her paper, including her wretched travel schedule, eventually took a toll as she began to suffer terrible migraines. The stress was getting to her—Dorothy had people depending on her, so many vulnerable people. Including Tamar. Especially Tamar. In later years, Dorothy would tell close friends that despite numerous failures and some deep tragedies, she had few regrets about the Catholic Worker. Her one regret was not having spent more time with Tamar during those heady formative years.

A common question people have about those dedicated to a life of radical welcome is how to do this faithfully in light of the constraints of family and family life. The answer for Dorothy was complex. Over the years, she consistently discouraged families from starting houses of hospitality, declaring it was almost fundamentally at odds with raising children in a safe and stable environment. Yet both she and Tamar also constantly spoke of the blessings of the interdependent life.

As the mother of two young children myself, it's important for me to take time to consider the complexities of hospitality in families. The beloved community of Dorothy Day and the Catholic Worker had its limitations—and in some respects is an indictment of the failure of their original vision. Peter Maurin and Dorothy thought every parish would start a house of hospitality for those who were destitute, but this never happened. The goal was never for Dorothy to live in community with poor people her whole life, but this is what ended up happening because others refused to extend welcome. In many ways, Tamar Teresa and her story show us these limitations and the downside of allowing one group to share all the burden of radical hospitality. Tamar was born into this community that so many uphold as the symbol of saintliness and Christlikeness. But she did not choose voluntary poverty or solidarity with those who were poor; it was chosen for her. She left the Worker community when she was eighteen and married a man twelve years her senior, whom she had met there. For the rest of her life, Tamar struggled financially, living a hardscrabble life on various decrepit farms with nine children to look after and feed.

Tamar, herself an only child, eventually became the mother of nine children. Dorothy, who had always longed for a house bursting with kids, became a beloved granny and great-granny in the later years of her life. This is how Tamar, the only biological child of Dorothy, likes to remember her. As a person, a woman, a mother, the creator of homes for those who had none: "In so many of her pictures, she looks stern and convent-like. Well, she wasn't that way at all, but was wonderfully warm and loving and created a real home for the poorest of the poor."[7] Her mother was no cardboard cutout of a grim saint, not a nun nor an absentee mother. Her mother was Dorothy Day, a whirlwind of contradictions. And someone, as Tamar's grandmother Grace Day would often remark, who often bit off more than she could chew.

Tamar never seemed to begrudge the countless people who claimed her mother as their own. She knew that the Catholic Worker was her mother's life's work. Tamar knew herself to be the daughter of a woman who started a revolutionary movement. She experienced the energy and electricity that accompany historic moments, even as she and her mother lived within the indignities of poverty. There were never enough blankets, there was never enough heat. Yes, the soup and the coffee pot were constantly on the stove, but the bedbugs were also a staple feature. But wherever Dorothy Day was, there was home—for Tamar and so many other people. Does that make Dorothy Day a saint? Whenever her daughter Kate asked her about this, Tamar would simply smile, refusing to answer. There was no simple answer to that big question. To be her daughter was to spend the rest of your life wondering what hit you, after all.

THE FARMS, THE WEEDS

As soon as the generals and the politicos
can predict the motions of your mind,
lose it. Leave it as a sign
to mark the false trail, the way
you didn't go. Be like the fox
who makes more tracks than necessary,
some in the wrong direction.
Practice resurrection.

—Wendell Berry, *The Mad Farmer Liberation Front*

I n 1935, Peter Maurin had been successful in two of his three-part
aims for restoring the world: the *Catholic Worker* newspaper and
the houses of hospitality. But he still longed for what he considered the most important part of his vision to come true: to have
a communal farm where people could go back to the land. Agronomic universities, he would grandly proclaim in his thick French
accent, were the future of society. As Dorothy traveled the country
reporting on labor issues and other injustices, Peter continued to
push for more than just pointing out the troubles of the world—he
wanted to build something better in the shell of the old empire.

He grew up in an agricultural village in France, where his family had farmed for forty generations. In his barn-home, animals lived on the first floor, and the humans lived on the second. His life and spiritual awakening happened in connection with the seasons of farm life, hard work, and religious indoctrination by local Catholic brothers. In contrast to his upbringing, he saw industrialization and capitalism as inherently dehumanizing and, as a result, inherently anti-Catholic.

For Peter, the farming communes would be the culmination of everything he and Dorothy were doing with the Catholic Worker: they would put forth a new vision of society, one where the laborer and the intellectual would come and work side by side in the fields and then spend the evenings discussing literature, theology, and philosophy. "Eight hours for work, eight hours for rest, eight hours for play," he wrote. Peter and the labor unions had something in common here: a philosophy of work that gave rights and dignity to people instead of working them to the bone and crushing them under the ideologies of profit and progress. He dreamed of good, honest work and taking care of everyone: those who were elderly, sick, and mentally ill. For him, that was all possible with the farm. "No one is unemployed on the land," he would tell Dorothy, his eyes sparkling behind cracked eyeglasses.

Dorothy was not so sure. Life at the Catholic Worker was going full tilt, and she could barely keep up with all her responsibilities and duties (and bills). But Peter was a wonderful propagandist and in time got all the young men who hung around the Catholic Worker house excited about the farm, both the hardened laborers and idealistic intellectual types. But Dorothy noticed that none of the women shared in the enthusiasm about this new venture. All that talk about hard, honest work hit them differently perhaps, as they continued to cook the meals and wash the dishes and clean the soiled linens of the house while the men smoked and talked about a utopian farming commune. "Everyone wants a revolution, but no one wants to do the dishes," reads a print I have hanging over my kitchen sink. Dorothy and the women who made up the backbone of the Worker knew this truth in their bones in ways that the men did not.

But Dorothy was open to Peter's ideas. As much as she loved the city—the hustle and bustle, the feeling of being at one with the masses—nature had always had a special place in her heart. It was at the beach where she learned to love a Creator God. She had an eye for trees and flowers and plants and their healing capacities, their ability to bring delight, and wrote about them often in her writings. Like many an idealist before and after her, the image of nature coexisting with the great gobs of people in a city caught her imagination—weeds growing up through the cobblestones in the city, the way her neighbors cultivated flowers to brighten up the tenement apartments.

Eventually, Dorothy caved, and through luck and donations from the paper, they purchased their first farm on Staten Island: only one acre and an eight-bedroom farmhouse not that far from the city. They grew vegetables in the garden and shared them with those living in the house in the city. The farm had a beautiful view of the bay, and Dorothy and others liked to come in the summer for the views and to escape from city life. Still, the Catholic Worker continued to attract all sorts of people, including those who made communal life rather difficult at times.

Peter's grandiose ideas about scholars and workers coming together to work the land and sit around and discuss ideas in the evenings didn't exactly work as promised. The class divide continued on even in an idealized, romanticized farm setting. People still needed to work the earth, weed the garden, do the dishes, make the beds, urge the "guests" (as they called the residents) to shower more than once a month, and be ever vigilant about bedbugs. But many simply wanted others to do those jobs while they sat around talking about their vision for a new society.

The farm on Staten Island only lasted for a year before money ran out. Dorothy might have been slightly relieved when the enterprise fizzled as she was smack in the middle of the golden ages of her newspaper, rushing around the country and accepting every invitation to speak.

The farm was more headaches and squabbles for her, but it wasn't too long before another opportunity came for a bigger piece of land in Pennsylvania seventy miles away. It was a large place they called Easton, and Peter was ecstatic. They bought it thanks to the contributions of a wealthy reader and dove headfirst into trying to wrestle it into a productive farm and communitarian housing. But the problems of a bunch of people running around and play acting at farming were made immediately clear: for one, it wasn't until after they bought the land that they realized there was no running water on the grounds, not even a well (water, it turns out, is rather essential to growing crops). The land they purchased had mounds of debris and trash in the soil, no real farm equipment, drafty and cold buildings uninhabitable in the winter—and nobody who knew what they were doing.

The thought of a bunch of happy Catholic radicals purchasing a farm with God's money, only to be stopped cold by practicalities such as access to running water. . . . It's almost funny, except if you were living through it.

One of the tensions of studying these early years of the Catholic Worker movement was Dorothy's tendency to wax romantic about the hard parts. In her own writings, especially the monthly newspaper, the official tone of the Catholic Worker movement was cheerful propaganda when it came to their endeavors. Everything was "a plucky experience" to be lived through. The farms were places where fresh fruits and vegetables were grown for the poor people living in the city, where people could come and relax and connect with God. Dorothy named the animals and wrote about them in her chatty columns—"George the goat broke into the house and slept on the beds!"—even as she left out the tensions with alcoholic guests, young men who hid stolen goods on the farm to support heroin habits, unpaid bills and lack of water, the backbreaking work and the helpless academics and professors sitting about telling others what to do. Unemployed and poor families were attracted to the farm, but just like the houses in the city, there was no perfect harmony to be found. Squabbles and fights and stealing happened regularly. A Catholic Worker farm was a place for people who couldn't fit in anywhere else, and relationships were often strained under the pressure of people in the throes of trauma or addiction.

On the farm, Dorothy said, they were actively trying to work out their ideas about the land being the solution to the problems of unemployment in the country. It was a real-time experiment—both exciting and heartbreaking. She wrote to *Catholic Worker* readers that they needed only six hundred dollars a year to keep the farm going. She juxtaposed the farm life with the Catholic Worker houses in the city and strove to make the connection for the readers:

> In the cities there is unemployment and the breadline. There are municipal lodging houses and the parks where men sit all day and are either sunk in lethargy or are racking their brains for a way out. And on the land there are untilled acres, there is room for every kind of employment where the single unemployed can pioneer and lead the way for the family, thus serving not only himself but the common good. While we work we pray that the farm at Easton and our writing about it will be so blessed that others will be led in this direction and do likewise. And in the many ways we fail, may they succeed, so that throughout the land there will grow up many communities within communities that will eventually save the nation from disaster.

It's hard to run a farm when nobody knows how to do it. It's hard to be in community with people who have been cast aside from society, even in the best of circumstances. It's hard to live in between the tension of the city and the farm, people pulling at you on all sides, bright ideas wilting like weeds in the hot sun of reality.

Easton eventually closed, even as other Catholic Worker farms sprung up in later years across the country. The farms didn't save the world, as it turns out, but Dorothy tried not to mind that so much. Planting the seeds of new ways to live life would take time, she knew. They were making tracks, sometimes in the wrong direction. They were practicing resurrection.

I love thinking about the Catholic Worker farms, especially the early ones. People with high ideals working without knowing what they were doing. Goats eating the crops, people refusing to work or bathe, an excess of turnips to be eaten. A group of starry-eyed Catholics buying an agronomic university that didn't even have access to water. The idea that a group of damaged and beautiful people plopped into the middle of a farm would turn into something that never resembled success. That it didn't work is entirely beside the point.

Or is it? There is a real possibility I am romanticizing these stories just as Dorothy did. I can't help but wonder if the farms wouldn't have failed if Peter and Dorothy would have been connected to—or sought—the wisdom of Indigenous neighbors and traditions related to justice and land. Peter, despite his family's generational connection to farming in France, did not seem to seek out and prioritize the original inhabitants of the lands now called Pennsylvania and New York State and their ways of cultivating the land. In the agronomic universities and the plucky farm experiments, in the disastrous attempts at creating a self-sustaining community, there was an ignorance or unwillingness to find the teachers they would need. Absent in the Catholic Worker were Native American advocacy, voices, and ideologies. That poverty of imagination shows itself in the farming experiments and beyond, where the vast stores of Native knowledge on honoring and stewarding the land were not engaged.

I think about this as I muck about in my small garden and as I read about the Catholic Worker farms in the 1930s and '40s that continue to exist to this day. How ignoring, or even romanticizing, bits of Indigenous wisdom without real engagement is an experiment in colonization. This is a part of my own cultural framework, and I see it in the early Catholic Worker farms as well.

Building beloved community is complicated, this we know, as is the collective history of the land in what we call the United States. We can acknowledge this, and the failures of the Catholic Worker farms, and see where similar narratives might be taking root in our own lives. One day, perhaps, it will be common knowledge to ask for Indigenous wisdom and expertise, to prioritize the voices long ignored in our society.

Peter, born on a poor farm in France, eventually did live out his dreams of farm life. When he was older, he lost his words, and he lost his ability to chant his Easy Essays. He sunk into silence, and the Catholic Worker community took care of him. His last years were spent on the Catholic Worker farm named Maryfarm, where he died peacefully in a little cottage. One man, one fox with no place of his own to lay his head, one bird of the air was given a safe place to be cared for in his last years.

As I consider Peter's vision of the land, I'm reminded of Genesis: life begins in a garden, humans and God and the animals and

the plants all living together in harmony. Flourishing together—
the original dream God had for the world. Dorothy, with her love
for the city and her desire to be amid the thrall of humanity, book-
ends that Genesis vision with one that appears in the New City in
the Book of Revelation. For Dorothy, heaven on earth was Italian
immigrants and their homemade plum wine, the songs and stories
of troubadours, the heady discussions of Russian novelists, German composers, and Black Pentecostal church services. Dorothy's
vision for a new way forward very much centered around cities
and living in a pluralized society that was hurtling pell-mell into a
new era of technology, liberation, and the opportunity for democracy and equality. Peter's was a view to origins, to the old and wise
ways of being in the world and God's original dreams as Creator
of the land. Both visions are beautiful, and complementary, and
necessary. And I'm thankful for the seeds Peter Maurin scattered
as he wandered through life. I pray even now that my heart would
be good soil for some of his ideas to take root, just like they did in
the person of Dorothy Day.

THE MYSTICAL, MYTHICAL BODY OF CHRIST

*Nothing does more harm to the progress of
Christianity and is more against its spirit than . . .
race prejudice amongst Christians.*

—**Jaques Maritain,** quoted in the January 1936 issue of the
Catholic Worker

W hen I immersed myself in the early archives of the *Catholic Worker* newspaper, I quickly noticed many of the articles were about race. In fact, the first five years of the *Catholic Worker* contains the most articles on race (in the context of Black Americans) in the history of the paper—it was evidently on Dorothy's mind, mostly related to labor issues. Even during the Civil Rights movement, Dorothy did not write as much about race as she did from 1933 to 1938, an average of three articles per issue.[2] The first *Catholic Worker* issue had a section near the front with the headline: "IS THE PROBLEM BLACK OR WHITE?" In it, she quotes a priest who wrote in *Commonweal*, "The problem is not what to do with the black man so much as it is what to do with the white man," which James Baldwin noted in similar ways and with fierce intentionality in the 1950s.

That same issue and article lists the very real discriminations facing Black people in 1933 in America. According to the *Catholic Worker*, they included being denied the right to vote, receiving lower wages than white co-laborers, and being charged higher rents than white people for the exact same housing. Black men couldn't join many trade unions and were denied from attending church with white folks. Schools were segregated everywhere but the North, and even there the educational system was unequal. Black people in the 1930s Jim Crow era were routinely barred from restaurants, hotels, and communal spaces—not just in the South, the article points out, but in the North as well. Black people did not receive the same rights or justice in the court of law, they had a hard time buying houses or getting a mortgage, and they were faced with violence when they lived in white spaces. They were brutalized by mob justice and public lynchings but were punished even harder if they sought to protect themselves from such terrors at the hands of white people. The *Catholic Worker* did not shy away from telling the truth about these matters, arraigning the inequality and injustice rampant in 1933.

That fall, a disgruntled Catholic came to the *Catholic Worker* office and calmly tried to explain why God made white people the superior race. In response, the editors wrote in the October issue, "The black man and the white man are by God's creation brethren, children of the same Father on earth and in heaven, redeemed alike by Jesus Christ and having equal rights." They go on to quote another Catholic priest, Fr. Gillis: "We are treating the Negro as unjustly, if not with quite so much bloody cruelty, as we treated the Indian. . . . We robbed the red man and killed him. But we kidnapped the Black man and enslaved him."

What was needed, the *Catholic Worker* piece noted, was confession, repentance, works of mercy, and social justice, in particular regarding Black Americans and all that continues to oppress them: "We recall a teacher of ours who used to say that as nations have no immortal souls they must be punished here on earth for their sins; and that this country will suffer deeply for its sins against the Negro." America, the *Worker* knew, would have to pay the price of the exploitation and oppression inflicted on an entire race of people. But Catholics perhaps could be uniquely positioned to offer the important act of penance: "If we cannot have perfect contrition for our sins, past and present, against the Negro, let us be moved through the imperfect contrition of our fear of retribution to work for justice for this bitterly oppressed tenth of our people." They saw in the United States a fundamental unwillingness to honestly repent for sins of racial injustice and racial terror in response to slavery and oppression of Black people—and this unwillingness was tied to a fear of retribution and the inability to conceptualize what real justice and reconciliation looked like.

Dorothy always knew that the United States had a poverty of imagination when it came to just economics—and she dipped her toe into the water of saying they had the same problem when it came to race. She was also aware that she was in the middle of a sort of culture war, as the communist party claimed it was the only one fighting for the rights of Black Americans. Dorothy, Peter, and several priests tried hard to make the case that true Catholicism was antiracist at its core, if only Catholics would live into their ideals and morals fully.

The *Catholic Worker*'s consistent writing about racism against Black Americans caught the attention of Dr. Arthur Falls, a prominent African American Catholic based in Chicago. He wrote to Dorothy to thank her and compliment her on the paper, even as he also pointed out that on the masthead of her paper, it showed two white workers. What if one of them were to be Black? Dorothy asked Ade Bethune to update the logo, and ever since the *Catholic Worker* has kept a Black worker on the masthead. In 2008, Bethune changed the white male worker in the logo to a farmworker woman carrying a child, to better reflect the times and the people most impacted by the issues facing our world.

Dorothy then invited Dr. Falls to contribute to the paper, and he occasionally wrote for them with updates on Chicago happenings. A surgeon involved in multiple groups for race relations in his city, Falls was excited by the idea of starting a school where one could have Peter Maurin's beloved roundtable discussions. While Peter focused in New York on bringing together the laborer and the intellectual, desegregation was the focus of Arthur Falls's aim with the Chicago Catholic Worker. Dr. Falls saw the need for integrated spaces of thought within the Catholic community and held out hope that his religious community could even be at the forefront of changing the social order in this realm as he envisioned bringing white and Black people of faith together. He was tired of being treated like a second-class Catholic, a new convert, or someone to be proselytized. Dr. Falls came from a long line of French Creole Catholics and drew on his rich history as he strove toward a vision of change and equality in his city.

Dr. Falls believed deeply in the radical nature of the doctrine of the mystical body of Christ—the idea that we are bound to one another as siblings, as parts of one body: "There is neither Jew nor Gentile, neither slave nor free, nor is there male and female, for you are all one in Christ Jesus."[3] And just like a body, there are many different parts and many different functions. But when one part suffers, it causes the rest to suffer. Falls noted that we are connected in our joy and suffering, and when someone in our community is suffering, the doctrine of the mystical body of Christ compels us to do something out of love and responsibility. In light of this mystery, being one with one another meant that issues of race or class should not hold people apart from each other.

Time and time again, Dr. Falls brought up the understanding of the mystical body of Christ to point out that doctrinally, racism and segregation were inherently anti-Catholic. Dr. Falls, Dorothy, and Peter knew that if this doctrine were taken seriously, it could and should reorder the world. Immediately.

No person would be left without shelter, food, and education.

Nobody would die alone on the streets.

Nobody would medicate their pain with alcohol or drugs.

Nobody would be resigned to spend the remainder of their days dying a slow death in a sanitarium.

And segregation and Jim Crow laws and radicalized terror through lynchings and more would be overturned in this radical reordering of the world.

Yet this didn't happen. Dr. Falls worked as tirelessly to erad-icate anti-Black racism as the saints of old battled their historic heresies. And he did it while living in a segregated neighborhood, staying stubbornly within the Church, and pointing out that *Catholic* meant "universal." But, as he remarked about Black folks in the Catholic Church, "'Universal' didn't mean us."[4]

Arthur, and so many other Black Catholics, time and time again saw the beautiful theology of inherent human dignity be dismissed in practical application. In the North, parish churches remained segregated, as well as in the South. Integrated Catho-lic Worker hospitality houses in cities like Baltimore were shut down and repossessed by city officials furious at the desegregation efforts, and sympathetic priests were punished for breaking seg-regation laws and reassigned elsewhere. Dr. Falls began to point out that white Catholics seemed to believe in a "mythical" body of Christ—one that was only for them.

Year after year throughout his life, Dr. Falls continued to work within his faith community, asking people if they truly believed the doctrines and teachings that pointed to equality before God. Even as many lauded Dorothy Day for remaining a faithful, devout Catholic until her death despite the opposition and trials she faced, the marvel of unrecognized saints like Dr. Falls—commit-ted Catholic and advocate for change despite treatment as a sec-ond-class citizen in the Church—is their unimaginable endurance, continuing day after day. His witness to the love of Christ for Black Americans in particular, even in view of the failure of the Church to convey the truth of that love in meaningful, societal ways, is a message that continues to be resonant, true, and necessary.[5] He pointed out the myth of unity within a white supremacist church. Almost one hundred years later, his moral clarity continues to be so sharp that it stings.

In the 1970s, Dorothy wrote several columns touching on issues of race and the history of the *Catholic Worker*. While she was proud the paper covered issues of exploitation of and injustice against Black people in its first years, she noted more recent attempts for Catholic Workers to learn from and study the writings of their Black neighbors, to hear of their backgrounds and history: "It is only these last years that we begin to realize how much we have studied all the histories save the histories of Africa and her peoples, and how little we have learned of the minorities in our own country."[6] While she overlooked W. E. B. Du Bois when they were both writing in the New York scene at the beginning of the century, at seventy, she started reading his work, writing that *The Souls of Black Folk* was "a good beginning in the study of African and American history in relation to slavery, past and present." Her recommendation for others, I believe, was her way of saying it was a good beginning book for herself—that she had so much to learn about the experience of being Black in America and the long-term effects of white supremacy in the American experiment.

We live in a world not so far removed from Jim Crow laws and segregated churches as we might life to think. Both Dr. Falls and Dorothy give us much to think about as we continue to wonder at what the mystical body of Christ would look like today. Dr. Falls so clearly saw the evil of racism in society and within the Church as he experienced it every day. Dorothy admitted only much later in life how much she simply didn't understand about the Black experience in America and how much she hoped to learn from those who were at the forefront of the struggle in her later years. For any person of faith, but especially those from privileged backgrounds, learning from marginalized communities about how to confront and address injustice is nonnegotiable. It is the only way to move forward.

Blessed are the meek, the poor, the oppressed. They will lead you, and you will learn from them all the days of your life. The mystical body of Christ that takes Jesus seriously honors those who know best the solutions to our problems, those who are blessed with true moral courage and eyes for justice. Those are the voices that workers in justice are called to listen for, listen to, and learn from to take action.

WAR AND VIOLENCE

O n the bombing of Hiroshima:

Mr. Truman was jubilant. President Truman. True man; what a strange name, come to think of it. We refer to Jesus Christ as true God and true Man. Truman is a true man of his time in that he was jubilant. He was not a son of God, brother of Christ, brother of the Japanese, jubilating as he did. He went from table to table on the cruiser which was bringing him home from the Big Three conference, telling the great news; "jubilant" the newspapers said. Jubilate Deo. We have killed 318,000 Japanese. That is, we hope we have killed them, the Associated Press, on page one, column one, of the Herald Tribune says. The effect is hoped for, not known. It is to be hoped they are vaporized, our Japanese brothers—men, women, and babies, scattered to the four winds, over the seven seas. Perhaps we will breathe their dust into our nostrils, feel them in the fog of New York on our faces, feel them in the rain on the hills of Easton. "Jubilate Deo. President Truman was jubilant. We have created. We have created destruction."

—**Dorothy Day** in the *Catholic Worker* editorial,
September 1, 1945

Blessed are the peacemakers,
for they will be called children of God.

—Matthew 5:9

In many ways, World War II ended the Great Depression. But at what cost to morality and the ethics of neighborliness? In a war, Dorothy wrote, nobody cares about human rights or dignity. It was her own caring that put her on the FBI watchlist, and the bureau ended up creating an extensive file for her. It received a tip alerting the authorities that Dorothy was writing in the *Catholic Worker* about Japanese internment camps on the West Coast and comparing them to German concentration camps. Dorothy Day was bad for morale. Dorothy Day was bad for the war effort. Dorothy Day was now officially on a watchlist.

She knew exactly what she was doing. In 1942, Dorothy Day traveled to Oregon and California and wrote about the grave injustices and systematic degradation happening to Japanese Americans in these states. Japanese Americans were forced to leave and sell their homes and businesses at a great loss (as other citizens and neighbors profited). She wrote of visiting the makeshift internment camp in Portland, seeing thousands of people behind barbed-wire fences. The few prisoners she could talk to on her trip shared the realities of their situation and their abject misery, and their desire to be set free. Japanese Americans were the first casualties of the war in the United States, Dorothy wrote. If she didn't write or agitate for their release, she said she would be failing at two of the works of mercy: to visit the imprisoned and to ransom the captive.[1] She would be a bad Catholic if she kept quiet.

The US government, now gearing up for additional war efforts in 1942, found Dorothy Day's perspective on internment camps dangerous. She continually ripped into the patriotic rhetoric of war and asked her readers to consider what they were being asked to do, as citizens, in the name of victory. What morals would they be forced to give up in order to "win"? She wondered how they could view their neighbors of Japanese descent with so little care or concern.

The violence of the militarized state and the phony patriotism of the war effort—Dorothy called out all of it. As I read Dorothy's column and immersed myself in her FBI files, I was shocked. I, who had lived on the outskirts of Portland, Oregon, for almost fifteen years, did not know that an internment camp had been set up inside my city, but it was true: thousands of Americans of Japanese descent had been held at what is now the Expo Center, a place I have been to multiple times for holiday bazaars and garden shows. In the main hall of the Expo Center is a plaque referencing the 1942 "forced housing" of over three thousand people of Japanese descent. I must have walked right by that plaque multiple times over the years. Just like I walked past houses and buildings and businesses that once belonged to the people forcibly removed and turned into prisoners of war in their own city, in their own country.

Dorothy's words shocked me awake. When she warned people about what going to war would do to their hearts and minds, she had a clear vision of Portland—my city—on her mind. Portland is a place where neighbors became enemies, simply because of their ethnicity, overnight. And the ramifications linger on, spiritually, socially, economically.

Dorothy did not write about Portland's beautiful rivers or the view of Mt. Hood or the friendly nature of our city. She wrote about the concentration camps we let be built in the center of our community. She wrote about how easily we accepted violence into our hearts and histories and whom it impacted the most. She wrote, in part, because she didn't want any of us to forget what it is like to be at war with your neighbors and how it is the people without power who will always suffer the most.

Her FBI file grew ever thicker in part because of the power of the ethical clarity she brought to undermining the war effort. Her writings asked people like me—comfortable, ignorant, privileged—to wonder just how much suffering the United States is willing to accept if it is done in the name of national safety and economic interests. If history tells us anything, it is that the amount of suffering is almost endless. And it is heretical to the way of Jesus. Dorothy said it during a World War, and its impact continues on. She said that we must pay attention to the lies of a nation at war and that we must also act.

Well before World War II and Germany dominated the headlines, Dorothy made her first real pacifist ripples when the Spanish Civil War started in 1936. She declared that the *Catholic Worker* was "sincerely a pacifist endeavor" in a time when the majority of Catholics in the United States were firmly on the side of Franco and the Nationalists in Spain. When Dorothy opposed the war and the tactics of the Catholic Franco, readers were shocked. In Franco, Dorothy saw the same brutal fascist authoritarian style of leadership that was being mirrored by both Adolf Hitler in Germany and Benito Mussolini in Italy in 1936. All three men claimed the Christian religion as one of their main talking points to rally people to their cause. Dorothy found Franco's Catholicism (similar to Mussolini's) to be a false faith and had no hesitancy in declaring that publicly.

For certain Catholics in the United States who longed to gain more power around the world and in their own country, Franco was not just a Catholic hoping to win Spain but also to simultaneously beat the communists—as the USSR was giving aid to Franco's detractors. As Dorothy spoke out, she aroused more suspicion within Catholic circles, surfacing questions around her supposed communist leanings.

In the 1930s, the *Catholic Worker* was not the only popular Catholic tabloid magazine in town. Conservative right-wing Catholics gained prominence in the cultural imagination through radio programs and newspapers of their own. Among the media voices was Father Charles Coughlin of Detroit, who was considered a very successful "radio priest." His reactionary stance to politics and pop culture is reminiscent of right-wing media today. He would whip his listeners and readers into a frenzy of fear against communists, Jewish people, African Americans, and more. In 1937, he came hard for Dorothy and the *Catholic Worker* in his own paper called *Social Justice*.[2] When the *Catholic Worker* failed to support Franco, and instead denounced him, Coughlin and many other Catholics began calling those at the helm of the newspaper communists in disguise.

Priests and archbishops started to censor the paper, canceling subscriptions and telling parishioners not to read it. The archbishop of Cincinnati, which had already banned the publication *Commonweal* for its stance on the war, refused to meet with Dorothy when she reached out. Instead, he sent her a letter stating that while he appreciated the voluntary poverty of the worker, Dorothy and her compatriots were simple laypeople without the right or authority to write or influence people around such big moral issues as war and pacifism.

The archbishop was right to be wary and concerned about the amount of power Dorothy wielded in the Catholic imagination at that time. Even with the troubles in Spain and being denounced by church leaders, readership of the *Catholic Worker* continued to soar, and in 1938, it was at its peak readership with almost two hundred thousand copies in circulation (an astonishing number now, it was even bigger back then among subscriptions and print media).

But Dorothy and Peter and others involved in the *Worker* knew that the trouble was only just beginning. While the Spanish Civil War caused Catholics in the United States to confront their own ideas about violence and religion and nation-states, the rest of the world was heading deeper into the conflicts that bloomed into World War II. Thanks to Peter, Dorothy was in communication and conversation with the first wave of people escaping Europe and emigrating to the United States, who shared the horrors happening in Germany and beyond.

Anti-Semitism was a staple of Catholic reactionary media at this time, and the *Catholic Worker* was aware of the rising levels of rhetoric and violence against Jewish people. The pope remained silent as Catholic nations like Spain and Italy passed laws against Jewish children attending public schools, and the cardinals in Poland actively stoked the fires of hatred, encouraging the boycott of all Jewish stores.

Dorothy was only just beginning to realize how much her pacifism rooted in the gospels of Jesus was going to cost her within the religion she herself had joined. Jesus was the ultimate example of someone who did not return violence with violence but loved his enemies to the end. This guiding principle infused her journalistic work. Pointing out the inconsistencies of both the church and the state during wartime was putting her at odds with Catholic leadership, with the US military and government, and with many of her friends, neighbors, and co-conspirators.

Dorothy, who maintained a lifelong interest in the issues and opinions of Jewish people in New York and beyond, found her pacifist stance in the late 1930s already causing her great grief—especially when she was accused of not caring about what happened to Jewish people under Hitler's regime. She did care, very much, and both she and Peter Maurin worked for ways to be in solidarity with Jewish people while also arguing that violence does not eradicate violence. In the *Catholic Worker,* Peter Maurin begged the US government to open its doors to Jewish refugees.[3] And in 1939, Dorothy helped form the Committee of Catholics to Fight Anti-Semitism, which resulted in many of those involved suffering job losses and status as the result of being on the committee.

But the United States entering World War II was going to change everything.

Dorothy and the New York Catholic Worker House had the almost unbearably difficult stance of advocating that the United States stay out of a war when a madman was murdering millions of people. For Dorothy and others in the Worker movement, the issues of pacifism and resisting the enthrallment of a wartime philosophy were connected to larger questions of what following Jesus looked like in the world and what kind of country the United States was going to be.

As the war progressed in Europe, and the United States geared up to join in, Dorothy was aware that the first step to fight was the mandatory conscription of young men into the military. In 1940, she testified before the House Committee on Military Affairs, asking the government not to pass a mandatory draft. This was personal for her as at that time there were few legal pathways in the United States for conscientious objectors. Catholic laypeople in particular had few options for resisting the draft due to religious exemption since the majority of Catholic hierarchy and leadership took a pro-war stance.

Dorothy's testimony didn't change the conscription process, and the draft bill was passed. But now Dorothy was officially on the radar of the US government as someone who was anti-war. In 1941, J. Edgar Hoover recommended that Dorothy be held by the United States for custodial detention in the case of a national emergency. The recommendation came after the July/August issue of the *Catholic Worker*, which opposed the compulsory military training bill. Now Dorothy was a person of interest to the FBI, as well as officially an enemy of the militarized state.[4]

It's unclear if Dorothy knew that, but she continued to oppose the draft and the war effort in general. To people in the movement, it looked like she was choosing pacifism as the one and only "gospel" issue for the community of Catholic Worker houses and newspapers springing up around the country. By 1940, there were over thirty Catholic Worker houses, with some even publishing their own newspapers, including the Chicago and Los Angeles workers. Many in these communities did not agree with Dorothy's pacifist stance on World War II, and some Worker communities started to refuse to pass out her newspaper. Dorothy was furious, meeting pushback on every level. She felt like even fellow Catholic Workers were now censoring her work and her views on pacifism, which she considered a central tenet of the movement.

Dorothy the anarchist then made the one and only true ultimatum of her Catholic Worker years: in a letter sent to all the other houses of hospitality, she said that if they were going to suppress her newspaper and the pacifist positions she put out, they should go ahead and break free of the Catholic Worker name. Those who had been so dazzled and inspired about Dorothy's view of voluntary poverty and works of mercy toward the poor read the letter with dismay and hurt. They felt strong-armed into supporting and publicizing views they disagreed with. Communities in Seattle and Chicago felt as though Dorothy's moral positions on war were putting all of their antipoverty work in jeopardy. If they promoted her newspaper, they would also be seen as traitors to the war effort.

Many tried to remind her that the Catholic Worker was more than just about pacifism. Peter remarked to her with sadness that men weren't ready for the radical nature of Christianity in wartime. Not only were they not ready, but they also simply didn't have a framework to listen and understand. Some accused her of being an inadvertent helper of anti-Semitic priests like Father Coughlin: to promote pacifism at this time was to let Hitler run wild. Even as Dorothy took in all of this criticism, plus the increasing surveillance put on her from both Catholic and government hierarchies, still she would not be moved. She clung to her pacifist stance while the readership of the paper plunged, and by the time the United States had officially entered the war in December of 1941, the *Catholic Worker* had lost over half of its readership, down to seventy-five thousand.

Almost everyone was angry with Dorothy. But she was taking a long view of the world, and humanity, and what being a Christian might ask of us. Among her astute observations back in 1936 was that the *Catholic Worker* didn't just oppose war or imperialism but also the increase of militarization in countries that engage in combat—what she called a "preparedness for war."[5] Because a country that prepares for war eventually goes to war, and the cycle continues on—with profits and the expansion of nation-states more valued than the human lives cost. The *Catholic Worker*, early on, asked readers to resist the ideological pull of forever preparing for war and becoming normalized to it.

In January 1942, one month after the United States officially being in the war, Dorothy wrote in her newspaper, "We are still pacifists. Our manifesto is the Sermon on the Mount, which means that we will try to be peacemakers." She goes on to say that the paper will be a voice for conscientious objectors and that "we will not participate in armed warfare or in making munitions, or by buying government bonds to prosecute the war, or in urging others to these efforts." Once again, her writing put Dorothy in hot water with both the US government and now with the cardinal of New York, who summoned her to his office, where she was told she could not tell people to avoid conscription into the army. (She acquiesced to his request but continued to write about pacifism.)

The war years were, by all accounts, a miserable time to be a sincere pacifist. But Dorothy found solace in her religious practices and in what it means to follow Jesus, a God who let himself be killed, only to be declared the ultimate victor over death. She hoped and prayed and lived as if victory over death and sin and war was a possibility in her lifetime. Peter Maurin saw how wars made enemies of men and how impossible it was to perform the works of mercy to all of humanity during organized conflict. He saw the world as forcing them to choose the lesser of two evils, to back violence in order to end violence. But Dorothy refused to make that choice, and she refused to let people believe her pacifism was a form of passivity.

In a world obsessed with power, national borders, and armed conflicts, World War II was the height of nationalism in the United States in many respects. And the *Catholic Worker* paper and the houses of hospitality themselves suffered for their stance against both conscription and military involvement in the war. When, in later years, they wrote about pacifism (especially related to Vietnam), they gained listeners as many more people asked questions about unchecked militarism and war efforts.

Throughout her life, Dorothy continued to ask the questions that looked not only at current events but the implications for the future: What does it do to a human soul to view another as the enemy and to kill them with ever more complex and terrifying weapons? What does it do to our souls if in order for our way of life to continue, we must view an entire country or race of people as the enemy to be vanquished instead of a neighbor to be loved and cared for?

The *Catholic Worker* newspaper never quite recovered from the hits it took during World War II. For the years and decades after the war, America was not ready to hear the radical call to live as if the Sermon on the Mount was real. Those who took Jesus's call to live as if every person was their neighbor were seen as enemies to the national war effort. But eventually more and more people became curious about living in ways that didn't fit into the American way of constant expansion, war, racism, and sexism. And Dorothy knew that even if most people disagreed with her, there was still an important role for her and others at the Catholic Worker to play. She wanted to keep a flame lit for people wondering how to break the cycles of war and oppression built into our histories and hearts.

How bleak would our world be if we didn't have a single sincere pacifist in it? Dorothy never expected everyone to agree with her. There are many communities, especially comprised of those who come from oppressed and marginalized groups, that have a lot to say in the dialogue about violence and what a Christian and justice-oriented response should be to oppression and war. But Dorothy saw herself as a testimony to the otherwise, a perhaps untenable way of being in the word that still pointed to God's dream for humanity. In her refusal to be practical, she saw it as one of her ways of sending up flares about the dream she shared with God.

A CONVERSION
OF PIETY

I always learn the hard way. It's the only way
I know how.

—Dorothy Day

O ne day, Kate Hennessy, daughter of Tamar and the youngest
grandchild of Dorothy Day, was rummaging around in her
mother's drawers when she found a stack of dresses. They were
colorful, flowery printed dresses from the 1920s and '30s. Tamar
would have been too small to wear these, so they must have been
Dorothy's. But these were not the drab, shapeless clothes that Kate
remembered her grandmother wearing. These flowery dresses
must have been the kind of clothes she wore before she started the
Catholic Worker.

The dresses, bright and vibrant, pointed to someone drawn
to beauty and life. But Dorothy put them away, right around the
time her life was upended by meeting Peter Maurin. Her friends
and family puzzled over the changes, and many who were close to
her became ever more amused and baffled as she developed the

reputation as a severe and unsmiling saint. They knew her as both that woman *and* one who loved colorful clothes and cute shoes and holding squishy babies and making her own dandelion wine. They tell us to remember that she had an infectious laugh and a wicked sense of humor and a taste for the finer things in life: literature, music, and plays in particular. And the reason the people closest to her—her only daughter, her grandchildren, people who came to the Worker and stayed many years—are desperate for people to understand a fuller picture of Dorothy is because this is the part of her that made people fall in love with her.

It wasn't just her ideals. It wasn't just her piety. It wasn't that she dressed like a saint long before the canonization process for her began. It was because, deep down, she was simply a person in love with the world.

In the stories from the people closest to Dorothy, including her family, there is the thread of wanting to hold on to all the parts that made Dorothy who she was. And she was somebody who eventually packed away her flowery dresses into a box, who went through periods of austerity and devotion where others could not follow her. She was somebody, just like all of us, searching for ways to have the strength to keep going in a world where she was overwhelmed by problems. And for a time, she thought the best way to move forward was to give up as many good things in the world as she could. This wounded those closest to her, who couldn't find themselves following Dorothy on her pilgrimage of piety. Tamar kept her mother's dresses, clothing Dorothy put aside when she came under the tutelage of a particular and rigid priest. What the daughter cherished, the mother packed away, never to be worn again.

The 1940s were a difficult decade for Dorothy Day and the *Catholic Worker*. The pacifist views Dorothy clung to made both the majority of her readers and the federal government nervous. Other Catholic Worker houses disagreed with her, some disbanding forever. Both the circulation rates and the number of houses of hospitality around the country were cut in half. After the chaotic early years and the never-ending lines of men and women looking for sustenance and clothes, the "guests" in various states of mental stability and physical cleanliness, the years of travel, the constant confrontations over war and religion and unions and pacifism, the schisms within the movement she created, Dorothy was spiritually, emotionally, and physically exhausted.

She had few people to look to for support as she struggled with her decisions and the realities of keeping the paper and the houses of hospitality going. As subscriptions and donations plummeted due to her pacifism and stance, Dorothy had the weight of all the bills on her shoulders—housing sometimes seventy long-term guests, feeding up to eight hundred people a day in the bread line, paying the mortgage on the farm at Easton, meeting the printing costs of the paper.

It was around this time that Peter left for several months, convinced that nobody at the Worker was listening to him or needed him, caught as they all were in the immediacy of the moment with strikes and war efforts. Dorothy didn't know how to reach him and appealed to him via her columns in the paper: "*Peter, please come back. We miss you, we really do.*" He was her ideological brother, the one who always reminded her of the loaves and fishes, of how God would come through in the most hopeless of moments. But then he left, and Dorothy was reminded again of how all the responsibility was on her.

Dorothy was dealing with her failures, professional, personal, and spiritual. She found solace in the life of Jesus, considered a failure by many, executed by the state and religious leaders. And she found solace in the belief that God could make a meal out of her meager offerings: "What we do is very little. But it is like the little boy with a few loaves and fishes. Christ took that little and increased it."[1]

It was during this intense period that Dorothy was introduced to several priests offering retreats to interested participants, all centered on an inward spiritual growth and an outward ethics of practice. Dorothy, who had previously not been a fan of such endeavors, quickly grew enamored. Especially by the work of one young priest named Father Hugo, who loved to say, "The best thing to do with the best things in life is to give them up." Dorothy asked Fr. Hugo and another priest to lead the retreat at Easton for multiple years in a row. It was a time of engagement and austerity, seven days when the participants were required to be silent and only listen to the priests delivering the lecture for several hours a day, with the rest of the time being spent in silent prayer and reflection or the reading of the gospels.

Dorothy relished the silence. She found the retreats strengthened her inner soul, even as others found the time oppressive, obsessed with giving up the "good things" of the world, and at odds with the God revealed in nature and creation. Stanley Vishnewski sat through the retreat, shook his head, and said, "What kind of a religion is this where God creates beauty and then tells you not to have it?"[2]

"The only good thing to come out of 'the retreat' was that Dorothy quit smoking," Tamar liked to say. Dorothy, who for years out of thrift and necessity had rolled her own cigarettes and chain-smoked them, quit cold turkey while under the direction of Fr. Hugo. He and his fellow priest who led the retreat had tried to get Dorothy to also give up coffee, but this turned out to be a bridge too far. Why, the Catholic Worker would crumble without coffee (Peter, ever the idealist, grumbled that coffee beans weren't local, and therefore one shouldn't be too dependent on the substance, but everyone ignored him). But cigarettes—yes, this was something Dorothy could strive to do for God. At forty-one, Dorothy prayed about it and gave up smoking. Tamar was pleased for her mother's health, but everything else about the retreat and how it affected Dorothy became a dark cloud that affected their relationship for years.

Tamar was sixteen when Dorothy became fixated on the retreat. In *The Long Loneliness*, Dorothy ends her book by describing Fr. Hugo and the retreat as her "second conversion." She found the intense nature of it spiritually strengthening and required all the people in her life to participate in it, much to their dismay. I can imagine Tamar attending, in sullen teenage silence, and listening with one eye on Fr. Hugo and another eye at the farmlands just beyond her reach. She would prefer to be with her goats and chickens and cats, or take a car ride with her mother in the countryside, or throw stones at the beach—all the places where she saw and experienced love and connection.

Instead, she had to sit and listen to a God who wanted her to give up all the good things of the world. The oppressive silence of the retreat was only broken by strange men telling her and the others what God wanted them to do. It didn't sit right with Tamar or many of the other retreatants. But Dorothy loved it, guzzled up every second of silence and every suggestion of what more she could give up to God.

The retreat was cruel, Tamar thought, a burden on the shoulders of those already in danger of being crushed by the weight of wanting to be obedient. The motley crew of the Catholic Worker had no trouble telling Dorothy she was alone in finding it restorative or as a helpful framework for life. Dorothy was used to people not understanding her turns toward God, which increased her sense of loneliness and her need to do the retreat more than ever. Ade Bethune aligned herself with teenage Tamar, telling Dorothy that the retreat didn't lead Ade to love God more at all. "Instead of focusing on struggling against yourself, simply find good things to do in the world and do them. That should give us enough to work on without parsing through every desire and giving up every little thing," Ade said.

The shy teenager Tamar grew more and more at odds with her mother during this time period. Her mother's "second conversion" seemed to take her away from everything Tamar loved about

Dorothy. Still, she tried her best to make her life in the Catholic Worker community as good as she could. Tamar had been bounced from school to school, never quite fitting in or making connections, but once the farm at Easton was purchased, she settled there on school breaks, taking care of a goat she purchased with her own money, and chickens, and various plants and flowers. In Dorothy's telling, the farm at Easton was a big lark in going back to the land and a place to hold spiritual retreats in silence and contemplation. For Tamar, it was a place where she wanted to try to find a bit of peace and stability in the midst of the whirl of the Catholic Worker life.

One story from those years struck me: Tamar saved up some money from her father and ended up enlisting the help of a fellow guest to build her own tiny house at Easton. When Dorothy, who had been off on a speaking tour, came to the farm and saw Tamar's new little house, she was dismayed—why, it was barely big enough for one bed! But this had been done on purpose—building Tamar a private residence so that it could only fit her and a visiting Dorothy and no one else. If there had been any extra room at all, Dorothy would have invited the next poor soul seeking lodging to bunk with them. Tamar deserved a little place of her own after all of those years of wandering.

I think about Tamar building her own little space on the farm that her mother wrote about so often in her paper. The farm where Dorothy invited priests to come and lecture for hours, telling everyone to try harder and give up more to follow God. Tamar refused this vision of a life of holiness, instead spending her money and her time and attention on the chickens and goats and flowers and vegetables.

Tamar, in her care for the world, reminds me that there are so many ways to love God, including loving the world. I wish Dorothy could have seen this during the retreat years. I believed she recognized Tamar's spirituality later in life as beautiful and restorative too. I know why Dorothy was drawn to the rigidity of Fr. Hugo, because it gave her a framework for how to be good. And what exhausted woman in their forties doesn't love the excuse for silence and space? But what Tamar and many others tried to tell Dorothy during those days was that there is a danger in saying only certain ways of living are holy. It damages us and turns the people we love into caricatures, one-dimensional. Plaster versions of saints instead of living, breathing, complicated people.

The story of the years of the retreats, of Dorothy becoming more religious and devout, is really the story of a mother and daughter growing apart. Until Kate Hennessy wrote about her mother and her grandmother's relationship, we only had Dorothy's side of the story regarding the years of her second conversion. Tamar, who did not like to publicly disagree with anyone, hated Fr. Hugo and his influence on her mother. She saw Dorothy's love of the retreat as a rejection of her and all the things that made Dorothy her mother. Her mother's little idiosyncrasies, like her love of cigarettes and radios and coffee and pie, her love of Staten Island and the beach and Broadway shows. A nice meal or silk stockings or a novel—all these things were now considered "of the world," and love for them should be interrogated at all times. Poor Tamar heard Fr. Hugo preach this repeatedly and watched her silent, beautiful, vibrant mother take copious notes. Tamar watched miserably as the retreat sharpened Dorothy's iron will to follow God and be devout. Tamar, trying to carve out her own little space in the world and on the farm, felt as though she was the ram being offered on a burnt altar to a voracious, demanding God. And she helplessly watched as Dorothy eagerly gave up all that was asked of her and more.

*T*he best thing to do with the best things in life is to give them up. Dorothy thought this to herself as she put away her rolling papers and loose tobacco for good. She must have put the dresses away around the same time. She organized and attended the retreat several times a year until Fr. Hugo and his fellow priests were eventually assigned elsewhere and punished for their teachings, which were considered extreme by most Catholics. Gradually, very gradually, Dorothy came to see how her asceticism and piety affected her relationships, how what she saw as good news felt like bad news to so many others struggling to know if they were even loved by God.

It wasn't the Catholic Worker houses, it wasn't the farms, it wasn't those who were poor and needy and the travel and the speaking and the strikes and the journalism. None of those made Tamar feel like she lost a mother. It was the retreat where she felt as if she lost Dorothy to a God who demanded detachment from everything that made the world such a delightful place to live in, including Tamar. It was during this time that, as she turned eighteen, Tamar got married to a difficult man many years her senior and moved to a succession of poor and overwhelming farms to manage. Her relationship with Dorothy was strained for many years. Much later, when Dorothy died, Fr. Hugo asked to speak at her funeral. When she heard this news, Tamar spat out that she wouldn't attend if that man was there. Even decades later, Tamar was furious at the priests who took her mother away from her.

For me, Tamar's anger is important to note. So, too, are all the people who knew Dorothy personally and who beg us not to put her on a pedestal, to view her simply as a saint. What Dorothy called her second conversion in *The Long Loneliness* later mellowed to simply another chapter in her long and storied life. Eventually, Dorothy stopped her pious phase. Tamar's nine children grew, and she eventually separated from her husband. And Dorothy and Tamar spent many a long week together, during those years of babies and old farms, rekindling their relationship. Kate Hennessy watched this all with the eyes of a small child growing older. She said she had never seen a love like that between her mother and her granny. They loved each other so fiercely. They disappointed each other, hurt each other, forgave each other. They clung to each other, perhaps making up for all those lost years in the middle.

Instead of looking to priests like Fr. Hugo for a retreat, later in life Dorothy would leave the bustle of the Catholic Worker and come be with her daughter. In whatever old farmhouse Tamar was living in, Dorothy would come and help take care of the children, sit in a rocking chair late into the night, read her Russian novels, and help with the chores. And somewhere in that house was a dresser full of Dorothy's old dresses, the ones she would never wear now—she was too old, too plain. But Tamar kept them as a secret, a side of her mother that the world never knew about. Both of them with gray hair, sensible dresses, sensible shoes. Sitting, and rocking, and loving each other in a mostly silent house. They would drink coffee, cup after cup of it. After all, they thought, why would God have made something so good and then ask you to give it up?

ALL THE WAYS
TO BE A SAINT

*People who live their everyday lives according to an
ideal are likely to make fools of themselves, which
is just what some critics think the Catholic workers
have been doing for nearly twenty years.*

—Dorothy Day

*I am not a saint. Unless you think of a saint as a
sinner who keeps on trying.*

—Nelson Mandela

Many people, from Nelson Mandela to Dr. King to Dorothy Day, have tried over and over again to tell us they were just one part of a community asking for change. They tried, and often failed, to subvert the narrative that they were singular, sole heroic persons. They knew what could happen when we baptize people as singular saints. Nelson Mandela knew it would erase his community and their history. Dr. King knew it would make him a martyr and a peaceful memory rather than a troubling one. Dorothy knew it meant that people wouldn't take her ideas about restructuring the world seriously. Turning someone into a saint means that we the onlookers view them as otherworldly. Different from us. We stare at them from a distance and marvel. But we do not wonder what we can and should do with our own lives in response to their ferocious witness to another way of being.

And this is what Dorothy wanted most of all.

Radical women like Dorothy are menaces to society, the church, and the government. They insist that the world change right now in order to prioritize those who are vulnerable. If even a handful of people decided to take Dorothy's advice seriously and perform the works of mercy with utter abandon, our society would collapse. Our economics, built on exploitation, greed, and hierarchy, would no longer be profitable. Our churches would change as those who are poor and meek and sorrowful would be the ones we turned to for wisdom and theology. No decision would be made without the awareness that every human being—especially the suffering one—is the image of Jesus Christ himself. We would not be able to simply accept our filthy rotten system anymore.

When canonized sainthood is discussed, it is determined within a hierarchy of power structures. And it is best to keep the tension between radical women and the Church in mind when sainthood is debated, when places of power try to find a place for people who never fit all too well into their molds, when radical people are sanitized by our adoration and veneration and our desire for them to be radical instead of us.

This is a common practice. Angela Davis reminds us that Nelson Mandela is now regarded as a worldwide symbol of nonviolent peaceful activism, a hero the world can look to, but until 2008, he was on the US terrorist watch list. Dr. King was assassinated right before preparing to preach a sermon on how America was going to hell for its sins of white supremacy. Similarly, in the future, Dorothy Day might simply become a woman who helped the poor, a conservative Catholic who stood for social justice, a saintly and safe jewel in the crown of American Catholic social teaching. But I hope this is not what happens. To do this disservice to Dorothy would be to the detriment of her story and how the saints—both canonized and not—shaped her life.

Here are a few of the things I love most about Dorothy Day:

She had a cat named Social Justice.

She had a ministry of praying for people who had died by suicide, confident that God's grace transcended time.

She was never too holy to give up coffee.

She liked perfume.

She complained about people constantly in her diaries.

She was a terrible driver but loved to clatter about in her succession of old, beat-up cars.

She refused to be good at public speaking.
She loved to read.
She wanted to be a saint,
and
she really, really didn't want people to treat her as one.

I t was when Dorothy was already in her seventies that Brian Terrell came to the Catholic Worker house in New York. His perspective—both as a Catholic and a co-laborer of Dorothy— offers a unique, important understanding of her own perspective on saints and sainthood. There is a quote often attributed to Dorothy that says "Don't call me a saint—I don't want to be dismissed that easily," but what she said to the *Chicago Tribune* in 1977 is even more pointed: "That's the way people try to dismiss you. If you're a saint, then you must be impractical and utopian, and nobody has to pay any attention to you. That kind of talk makes me sick." From his few years working alongside her at the Catholic Worker, Terrell knew Dorothy took the saints very, very seriously. And not just the ones the Catholic Church officially deemed saints. Terrell mentions Dorothy's lifelong habit of honoring and collecting a wide array of characters, both real and novelized, as people to look upon for wisdom, inspiration, and emulation. Be it St. Therese of Lisieux or Father Zosima from *The Brothers Karamazov* or the person in the Catholic Worker house that day having a mental break from reality, Dorothy was able to find something of the image of God in that individual and honor it by her deep reflection and attention on them.

Terrell also remembers living at the Catholic Worker house the last few years that Dorothy was alive and how irritated she was at the people who came by to meet her and gawk upon her as a "living saint." If they cared about her, then they would care about the people working, serving, and living at the Catholic Worker, she grumbled. She knew even then the dangers of a cult of personality forming around her.

The US bishops who voted unanimously to move forward with Dorothy's canonization process in 2012 and framed her life pre-conversion as one of "sexual immorality, religious searching, pregnancy out of wedlock and an abortion."[1] Archbishop of New York Cardinal Dolan, who boasts about being close friends with Donald Trump, paints Dorothy as someone who as soon as she converted to the Catholic Church, everything in her life was changed for the better. According to Cardinal Francis George, she became a pioneer in resisting the welfare state and is a "champion of conservative ideals." These cardinals mention Dorothy's assured ideological "battle against the Obama administration's contraception mandate and endorsement of gay rights." And they said, "As we struggle at this opportune moment to try to show how we are losing our freedoms in the name of individual rights, Dorothy Day is a good woman to have on our side."[2] The way these conservative leaders deal with Dorothy's pacifism and anarchist leanings is almost masterful. The Church needed a few pacifists like Dorothy just like society needed a few single, celibate people—outliers who teach us something useful, even as the leaders themselves reject pacifism and "recognize there are just wars because governments must defend their citizens."[3] Regarding Dorothy Day's response to "the injustices of capitalism," Cardinal George wrote, she simply practiced the works of mercy, which we should all do. No talk of reordering or restructuring a society that leads to such large amounts of poverty and misery.

Cardinal George's is among the many examples of a revisionist history of Dorothy Day, which attempts to capitalize on her life—and the lives of other radical Christians—to further their own aims. In George's case, it is political: a Dorothy fashioned on "their" side as someone who would rage against gay rights and abortion and where her work of anti-capitalism, anti-militarism, anti-patriarchal hierarchy, and so much more is largely ignored.

But Dorothy Day did not live and work and pour her life into the Catholic Worker in order to defend the rights of the Church. She didn't practice the works of mercy simply as a response to the injustices of capitalism; she practiced feeding, clothing, and taking care of her neighbor and also demanded that another economic system was required if one wanted to live out the gospel.

She fiercely believed there was never a just war, never a reason for a country to engage in violence against another. She lost many readers and supporters because of her opinions—a readership lost in part because of church hierarchy denouncing her views. Dorothy suffered for her radicalism during her life, because that is what truly countercultural ideals invite. To pretend she is not a radical is to erase Dorothy's story. She is unruly, in all the best ways, but longed for her views to be the norm. This, more than anything, is what makes her so dangerous to people in power.

✶

There are many valid responses to the idea of Dorothy Day being a canonized saint—close friends of hers like Robert Ellsberg are highly enthusiastic at the prospect and are intimately involved with the process. To have such a radical woman to look up to as a canonized saint is thrilling indeed and would ensure more people know her name and story. But as a non-Catholic myself, I sometimes imagine Dorothy having mixed feelings about it all. In the same way I think Dorothy would frown at the prints I have of her face on my walls or the t-shirt I wear with her saying "What we would like to do is change the world." She would be amused to have a ferry in Staten Island named after her (*At least it's free*, I imagine her saying). She would perhaps be astonished at the number of books written about her. And she would laugh at how still so few know her name and her story (remember the journalists in Washington, DC during the pope's address to Congress?). Dorothy is right in the thick of it all, known and unknown, mysterious and inscrutable and down to earth and solid. She truly did long to be a saint even as she fiercely objected to any attempts at putting her on a pedestal. She saw the divine image of God, a halo shimmering behind the faces of the men lining the streets of the Bowery, in the confused souls who poured into the Catholic Worker to find their vocation, in the protagonists in her favorite Russian novels. And she even saw saints inside the hierarchy of the Church.

She loved the canonized saints even as she kept a healthy distrust of those who made them official. Dorothy once wrote, "In all history popes and bishops and father abbots seem to have been blind and power loving and greedy. I never expected leadership from them. It is the saints that keep appearing all through history who keep things going." She struggled almost constantly with her relationship to the authority figures of the church. But she never stopped falling in love, over and over again, with the people she met every day. The unsung saints, the people who lived and died in almost complete invisibility to the powers that be, Christ himself showing up in these unlikely disguises.

She loved the saints. *Canonize me*, I can imagine her saying. *And canonize everyone else too.*

In 1949, when Peter Maurin died and was buried in a suit someone else had cast aside and in a donated grave, *Time* magazine reported on his death—calling it fitting and proper for a man known for his love of voluntary poverty. They noted the people who lined up to pray over his casket, to reach out their hands to touch him. His funeral had the air of one of the saints, and people lined up for a blessing.[4]

Born a poor son of peasants, he died poor, with little to his name in terms of worldly success. His mind had been failing for some time, and his last five years were lived out mostly in silence. "I've forgotten my words," he would respond to people who spoke to him. But he was cared for, day and night, by kindly Catholic Worker folks and died peacefully on a borrowed bed on the Maryhouse farm. People lined up to come to his funeral, bishops and lay Catholics and New York neighbors alike.

Dorothy mourned Peter. Without him, she was lonely in a new way. His longing for God cheered her up on her most depressing days. At the time of his death in 1949, Dorothy had been running the Catholic Worker movement for sixteen years. Her daughter was now grown and married. People had come to the Worker and left the Worker. Several Worker groups turned into a cult and tried to take over one of the farms. She weathered World War II, barely. She had found solace in the retreat with Fr. Hugo and had stopped smoking several years ago. And the Catholic Worker continued to serve soup and coffee and bread to lines of people in New York City.

Now it was no longer the men who thronged the streets looking for work in the Great Depression. After the war, the demographics of poverty shifted and changed. As more and more people of color were barred from accessing the GI Bill and other subsidies, and as more veterans and others suffered from mental illness and addiction, these became the hallmarks of many of the guests of Dorothy and the Worker.

Dorothy wrote and then published *The Long Loneliness*, which would become a bestseller and make herself and her work more visible than ever. By this point, her hair was almost white as the snow, even as she carried the energy of a much younger woman. As she wrote, she tried to immerse herself in the before times, her youth and her conversion to Catholicism and the start of the *Worker*. The *New Yorker* reached out for an extensive profile on her, and she agreed—but she herself sat down with a copy of the profile and edited out all the parts she wished to remain hidden.[5] Inscrutable, unruly, and possessive of her life and her work, she saw how God can use anyone and any situation to work God's will but still struggled to believe this of herself.

In the context of her life up until the 1950s, I think about the word *loneliness* and how important the concept was to her. *When you ask why, you are alone*, I can imagine her thinking. Even at a very young age, Dorothy seemed to sense this. When you live in a country that depends on obedience, nationalism, and militarism, asking why is a terrible sin. When you want to follow God but ask why so many Christians neglect the fundamentals of the gospel—to feed the hungry, clothe the naked, visit those sick and imprisoned, and to do away with a society that creates such need— you are lonely as you are ignored or called a heretic. Dorothy was always trying to find others who also asked why; her writings and her readings reflect this fundamental curiosity, this longing to know why the world was not how it should be. She was always sending up flares, trying to find fellow pilgrims and seekers and question-askers. I am so happy she did. I am one of the lucky few who found her and her words and her questions, and my life has never been the same.

Dorothy Day's obituary, like that of many famous people, had already been partially written before she died. In the New York world, she was a known person and had been from the time she was a young bohemian to her many decades of life in the various Catholic Worker houses. For years, the sitting draft of her obituary was tagged with the simple note "page one." Her life, and death, would be front page newsworthy.

At her funeral, Tamar was there, with her children and grandchildren filling many seats. Forster helped carry the coffin down the aisle—in the later years of her life, Dorothy and Forster had grown close again, to the point where they talked to each other almost every day on the phone. Ade Bethune, still making art for the *Catholic Worker* all those decades since the start, and so many others were there—people who had lived or volunteered at the Worker, guests and helpers and editors and friends. Communists, socialists, leftists, priests, pious old ladies, and people under the influence of various substances. All of them gathered together because she drew those disparate groups toward herself and gave them a wider community.

On Dorothy Day's grave is a drawing of loaves and fishes and the words *Deo Gratias*. Her tombstone tells us so much about her life. Calling us back to the biblical story of Jesus feeding the five thousand with loaves and fishes. It is a story reminding us of God's provision. On her grave, she wanted a reminder that she expected miracles and that she carried the duty of delight and of gratitude to God. At the end, she wanted to say she was thankful for everything, absolutely everything, in her long, storied, often lonely and hard life.

Canonized saint or not, Dorothy is someone I turn to in times of need, someone who provides me comfort and sustenance and helps me envision a future where I can still be a Christian, despite the hypocrisy and betrayal I have experienced in the Church. One of my Catholic friends told me I already treat her like one, a friend to turn to when I myself am overwhelmed by the injustice of the world. She is the person I read when I need to be reminded that an economy that prioritizes profits over people is antichrist. She's who I turn to when I want to be inspired by someone who married

Christian theology with direct action. She's who I look to when I realize my soul is parched and I long to be renewed and filled with the love of God in order to keep going. Already, for me, she's a saint of sorts, one of many radical women who have upended my life and who encourage me to keep making, as the late John Lewis would say, good trouble. She is among the contradictory, grumpy, hilarious, profound, pious, unruly—and necessary—women I look up to. Whatever box I try to create for her, she slips through, showing yet another surprising side to her.

More than anything, though, Dorothy Day is someone who makes me feel less lonely in this life. She was a holy fool determined to shame the wise. She is, and always was, the perfect mix of the profane and the sacred. She was a human, a mother, a sister, a daughter, a comrade, a muckraker. She was a sinner who kept on trying. I hope she knows now how not alone she is, in a great cloud of witnesses that includes muckrakers, pacifists, radicals, visionaries, and the poor in spirit.

She is one of the ancestors who guides us, cigarette in one hand and a cup of coffee in the other, saying to us, *Never stop asking why, and never stop hungering for God. The loaves and fishes will miraculously appear, but only if you surround yourself with those who are hungry.*

THE STORY OF A MOVEMENT, THE STORY OF HUNGER

Oppression in any of its forms means death. . . .
Liberation brings life. God liberates because God is
the God of life.

—**Gustavo Gutierrez**, *The God of Life*

In 1985, Pope John Paul II went to a shantytown in Peru to meet with the faithful who were desperate for a better world. Two local representatives of the community spoke before him: *Holy Father, we are hungry. We struggle for life in the midst of death.* Tuberculosis, wages of less than twenty-five cents a day, overcrowding, the lack of food—they experienced it all. The representatives from the community spoke to the pope as he sat on a mat of reeds deep in the shantytown built to accommodate those who were poor and oppressed and looking for survival. As Gustavo Gutierrez wrote about this encounter, he focused on how the pope responded. Surrounded by the great need, by the death that human forces both created and suffered, this is what the pope said: "I want this hunger for God to remain but I want the hunger for bread to be satisfied; I want means to be found to supply this bread. I want there to be none who go hungry for daily bread: People should be hungry for God but not starved for their daily bread."

He said this to crowds who experienced both, and the applause was thunderous. The poor knew intrinsically that "faith and starvation cannot be combined, because the God of Jesus is the God of life, of all life. Because of their experience, the believing poor grasp the point clearly. . . . We take the name of the Lord in vain when we appeal to God in order to justify and induce forgetfulness of the mistreatment of the poor."[1]

When I read Gustavo Gutierrez's record of this meeting of the pope with the poor, it sparked something within me. We do not have to accept the world as it is, full of hunger, homelessness, police brutality, tear gas, domestic violence, addiction, abuse, wealth inequality, deaths from COVID-19 and other pandemics. And we do not accept it precisely because we are people who believe in the God of life. We resist the work of death in everything that we do. Not in spite of being Christians but because of it.

D orothy Day carried profound hunger within her. She was someone constantly hungry for God. She was also hungry for everyone around her to have enough bread. These deep desires, forever working together in beautiful ways, birthed a movement that continues to this day. Those who have been impacted by the Catholic Worker testify to this—so, too, do the countless others like myself who have been radically changed by reading the works of Dorothy Day and following her call and vision.

By necessity, this book had to narrow in on one specific part of Dorothy Day: the founding of the Catholic Worker. In that sense, it really is a book about the birth of a movement. As such, it follows the flow: the background, the heat of starting something new in order to confront problems, and the necessary complications and wider perspectives needed as the movement gained strength and years.

I loved spending time with Dorothy in the 1930s, when she was nearing four decades of life. I was captivated by looking at black-and-white pictures of the Bowery and the men lining up for soup and coffee. I found myself constantly thinking about the United States during the flu of 1918 and the Great Depression and the New Deal and World War II. But most of all, I loved immersing myself in the stories surrounding the birth of a movement, the heady excitement of the *Catholic Worker* newspaper, and the houses of hospitality starting.

But movements grow up and change and morph—becoming more complex and transforming as time marches on. Dorothy's life did not end when this book did, and she continued to have a long and storied life of voluntary poverty and solidarity with those who were poor and to write about it.[2] The Catholic Worker exists until this day—both the paper (which you can subscribe to for twenty-five cents!) and a multiplicity of houses of hospitality throughout the world. Of course, it looks different than it did in the 1930s, and new questions continue to be asked of both the movement and the people it seeks to serve as we enter into new eras.

When it comes to writing about historical figures and figures we admire, it can be difficult to know how to ask the fraught questions: Where was Dorothy Day on the topic of race? Where was she on the spectrum of human sexuality or gender identity, on neurodivergent or disabled voices? These aren't questions designed to force her into the present but, in reality, are tied to her theology, which was formed in the 1930s. Just like Dr. Falls tried to point out nearly a century ago, we can ask ourselves: do we really believe we are all one in that mystical body of Christ—Black brothers and sisters, Indigenous and Latinx and various other immigrant and marginalized communities harmed and disregarded by the Church?

Dorothy covered labor issues for decades and saw firsthand that those in the thick of the struggle were rarely satisfied by the small amounts of change they saw happen. But over time, Dorothy saw how progress was made—child labor laws and better working conditions for women, the right to vote, increased unionization. I think about what this means for those of us who feel tired in the struggle for justice. Where can we see signs of change coming?

Gay Catholics, like journalist Michael J. O'Laughlin, have been reporting for over a decade on the changing perceptions of Catholics when it comes to issues of sexuality. From 2010 to 2021, there was a 20 percent jump, from 49 to 69 percent, in US Catholics advocating for civil rights and same-sex marriage to be legal.[3] The majority of Catholics, including Latinx Catholics, are now affirming of same-sex marriage, even as the "official" position of the Church contradicts these findings. O'Loughlin, while creating a podcast and book covering the untold stories of the AIDS crisis and the Catholic Church, found so many LGBTQIA+ people who continued to identify with the Catholic Church or Christianity in general. Their reason? It was in the Church they learned of their inherent dignity and the dignity of all people. The mythical body of Christ, connected to one another. This reality, more than the policies enacted from the leaders on high, impacted their lives.

We can only see the enormity of the situation and conversely celebrate the good work by listening to the people most impacted by evil. We will only ever discover if the Sermon on the Mount is being realized in our cities when we start to listen to those who are poor, meek, sick, and sad. Those who hunger and thirst for their daily bread and those who hunger and thirst for justice. When they are satisfied, we will know we live in a world where it is truly easier to do good.

Robert Ellsberg, friend to Dorothy and editor of the *Catholic Worker* in the '70s, likes to say the Catholic Worker movement is like a soup—similar to the stews the Catholic Worker had simmering—and still does to this day—at all hours of the evening. The soup of the Catholic Worker, says Ellsberg, is made up of the works of mercy outlined in Matthew 25. Christ, he says, comes to us disguised in the needs of our neighbor: those hungry, sick, and homeless. Our call is to meet those needs, and many people around the world commit themselves to these works of mercy. But the second ingredient that makes the Catholic Worker soup unique is calling attention to, protesting, and resisting the systems, the culture, and the values that give rise to so much poverty and need. And this is a ministry we very much need today.

We are in a time of great unveiling, a time of revelations. As such, we are also entering a time for new movements to be birthed. While I remain despairing at much in the world, I find solace and hope in seeing places of growth. In my own city, I see mutual aid efforts and protests organized against brutality, people banding together to take care of each other. I see more and more people listening to voices that have been silenced and marginalized both within Christianity and within society as a whole: LGBTQIA+ Christians, Latinx neighbors, Black and Indigenous voices, refugees and immigrants, those disabled and neurodivergent. And I find people, throughout history, who continually show me that a life of Christianity and a life where justice is pursued are not mutually exclusive. In fact, I find people who show me that I am not alone in feeling like the only way I can make sense of my life is to pursue Jesus to the edges of society and pitch my tent with the other outsiders.

Dorothy Day is one of those people who gives me enormous amounts of hope for my future and for my own complicated personhood in my own complicated country. She was not a perfect person, nor do I think she ever claimed to be. And for all of her foibles and blind spots, she was able to become more curious about the world, instead of less, the older she got. Love is the answer, she said, and I believe her based on how she tried to keep loving her neighbors until the very end. And this—this is what I want for myself most of all.

I hope I remember this as I make my own mistakes and must learn to lament, confess, and repent of the ways I have not loved my neighbor well. I hope I am lucky enough that when I am at the end of my life, like Dorothy, I will be able to clearly say how little I knew about the lived experience of others, especially those who have been disenfranchised on purpose. I hope I will not view myself as the only person who knows what is right in the world, and I hope I learn to seek answers for the world's problems outside of myself. I hope I learn to prioritize the people in my neighborhood who are struggling mightily to survive in America—their voices, their stories—and, most of all, look to them to tell me how to move forward, both as a follower of Christ and as an American.

The people our culture has cast aside, the ones the status quo has never listened to—these are the people Dorothy Day sought out. She never aimed to be the mother of a movement. She was just hoping, always hoping, that everyone else would shift their eyes to the margins. The Catholic Worker community was never meant to be an icon of beloved community, something to read about and marvel over. It was supposed to be a way of life for the Christian committed to living out the ideals of their beloved savior. Her typewriter, her tenement apartments, her soup and bread lines—they were all ways of trying to address the needs of the day while also sending up a flare to find fellow companions on the long, often lonely, journey.

May we continue to hunger for God but ensure our neighbors never hunger for bread. May we believe in love. May we believe in a God of life. And may we find each other on this journey, committed to it being long but not quite so lonely as we thought it would be.

FURTHER READING

Dorothy in Her Own Words

Day, Dorothy. *From Union Square to Rome*. Maryknoll, NY: Orbis Books, 2006.

Day, Dorothy. *House of Hospitality*. Huntington, IN: Our Sunday Visitor Publishing Division, 2015.

Day, Dorothy. *Loaves and Fishes*. Maryknoll, NY: Orbis Books, 1997.

Day, Dorothy. *The Long Loneliness*. New York: Harper Collins, 1997 edition.

Day, Dorothy, and Robert Ellsberg. *All the Way to Heaven: The Selected Letters of Dorothy Day*. New York: Image Books, 2012.

Day, Dorothy, and Robert Ellsberg. *Dorothy Day, Selected Writings: By Little and by Little*. Maryknoll, NY: Orbis Books, 2015.

Day, Dorothy, and Robert Ellsberg. *The Duty of Delight: The Diaries of Dorothy Day*. New York: Image Books, 2011.

To access the early issues of the Catholic Worker newspaper, go here: The Thomas Merton Center at Bellarmine University. "Sub-Section H.17a, Zarrella Papers: Catholic Worker Newspapers." Accessed February 4, 2022. http://www.merton.org/Research /Manuscripts/CW/.

Other Recommended Reads

Cone, James H. *Speaking the Truth: Ecumenism, Liberation, and Black Theology.* Grand Rapids, MI: Eerdmans, 1986.

Cornell, Thomas C., Robert Ellsberg, and Jim Forest. *A Penny a Copy: Readings from the Catholic Worker.* Maryknoll, NY: Orbis Books, 1995.

Cowley, Malcolm. *Exile's Return.* Viking Press, 1951.

Ellul, Jacques, and G. W. Bromiley. *Anarchy and Christianity.* Eugene, OR: Wipf & Stock, 2011.

Forest, Jim. *All Is Grace: A Biography of Dorothy Day.* Maryknoll, NY: Orbis Books, 2017.

Gustavo, Gutiérrez, and Matthew J. O'Connell. *The God of Life.* Maryknoll, NY: Orbis Books, 1991.

Hennessy, Kate. *Dorothy Day: The World Will Be Saved by Beauty.* New York: Scribner, 2017.

Loughery, John, and Blythe Randolph. *Dorothy Day: Dissenting Voice of the American Century.* New York: Simon & Schuster Paperbacks, 2021.

Maurin, Peter, and Lincoln Rice. *The Forgotten Radical Peter Maurin: Easy Essays from the Catholic Worker.* New York: Fordham University Press, 2020.

McCarthy, David Matzko. *The Heart of Catholic Social Teaching: Its Origins and Contemporary Significance.* Grand Rapids, MI: Brazos Press, 2009.

Piehl, Mel. *Breaking Bread: The Catholic Worker and the Origin of Catholic Radicalism in America.* Tuscaloosa: University of Alabama Press, 2006.

Rice, L. *Healing the Racial Divide: A Catholic Racial Justice Framework Inspired by Dr. Arthur Falls.* Eugene, OR: Pickwick Publications, 2014.

Riegle, Rosalie G. *Dorothy Day: Portraits by Those Who Knew Her.* Maryknoll, NY: Orbis Books, 2006.

Terkel, Studs. *Hard Times: An Oral History of the Great Depression.* New York: Pantheon Books, 1970.

Thurman, Howard. *Jesus and the Disinherited.* Boston: Beacon Press, 2022.

ACKNOWLEDGMENTS

I signed the contract to write this book in March 2020, confident I would have all the time in the world to settle in and write a book about one of my favorite people. I ended up writing this book in the snatches of time I could find while trying to parent two young kids during a global pandemic that upended everything about our lives. If you are a caregiver to young humans, then you probably have a good idea of how difficult this ended up being for me. I want to acknowledge all of us, all of us, who were able to get anything done during unprecedented times. I thought a lot about Dorothy, who did the best she could with her limited time and resources and hoped it did some good in the world. I'm thankful for her witness in so many ways. Including what it is like to be a harried mother writing while the world seems to crumble around you.

I want to say thank you first and foremost to my husband, Krispin, who did everything humanly possible to help and support me. The love of my life has listened to me talk about Dorothy Day for many, many years. I am sure he is pleased that now I will have other people to talk to about her.

Thank you to Rachelle Gardner for helping me land this proposal, and to Lil Copan and the team at Broadleaf for taking a chance on an unruly saint. I had so many people help me during the writing and researching of this book: Adam McInturf at Windows Booksellers continues to be a wonderful reference librarian and help. I'm grateful to Phil Runkle at the Marquette University Catholic Worker Collection archives and to Kate Hennessy for her email correspondence and insights. Historian Lincoln Rice was wonderfully patient with my questions. Robert Ellsberg showed me such kindness and such a careful reading of my book. I am indebted to him and his graciousness. Brian Terrell has an encyclopedic memory of everything Dorothy Day has ever written, and he has taught me so much about the Catholic Worker community. I reached out to scholars hoping for feedback and came away with friends whom I deeply admire.

I'm grateful to my writer friends and activist friends who encouraged me along the way: Kelley Nikondeha, Amy Peterson, Stina Kielsmeier-Cook, Jessica Goudeau, Christiana Peterson. Thank you to my family, my pod. There are so many people who have encouraged me along the way, and I want to thank you all. We have all known the long loneliness of these past few years. Together we will crawl toward a new kind of community, one where it is easier to help take care of each other. Thank you to everyone who has modeled this for me, who has gifted me with the ministry of delight and hope in hard times. Thank you, thank you, thank you.

NOTES

Introduction

1. She, and the Catholic Worker, did pay local taxes.
2. From the epigraph of *The Long Loneliness*.

Part 1 The Beginning Years

Our Lady of Perpetual Conversions

1. Day, Dorothy. *From Union Square to Rome* (New York: Arno Press, 1978), 1938. https://www.catholicworker.org/dorothyday /articles/201.html.
2. Day, Dorothy. *The Long Loneliness* (New York: Harper Collins, 1997 edition), 45.
3. Day, *Long Loneliness*, 39.
4. Day, Dorothy. *From Union Square to Rome, 1938* (Creative Media Partners, LLC, 2021). Accessed here: https://www.catholicworker .org/dorothyday/articles/204-plain.htm.

Muckrakers

1. "I Aimed for the Public's Heart, and . . . Hit It in the Stomach." *Chicago Tribune*. January 1, 1970. Accessed here: https://www .chicagotribune.com/news/ct-xpm-2006-05-21-0605210414-story .html.
2. According to Della, Dorothy's sister.

3. *The Masses* had urged people to resist conscription efforts, which did not please the federal government.
4. Psalm 130.

The Lost Generation

1. Stein, and many others, completely discounted the subsequent Harlem Renaissance happening in New York City, but it is important to note the overlap in timeframes.
2. Cowley, Malcolm. *Exile's Return* (London: Penguin Books New Ed, 1976 edition), 8.
3. Cowley, *Exile's Return*, 69.
4. Loughery, John, and Blythe Randolph. *Dorothy Day: Dissenting Voice of the American Century* (New York: Simon & Schuster Paperbacks, 2021), 73.
5. Hennessy, Kate. *Dorothy Day: The World Will Be Saved by Beauty* (New York: Scribner, 2017), 23–25.
6. Day, *Long Loneliness*, 94.
7. Loughery and Randolph, *Dorothy Day*, 79.
8. Terrell, Brian. "Dorothy Day: 'We Are Not Going into the Subject Matter of Birth Control at All as a Matter of Fact.'" *National Catholic Reporter*. September 30, 2015. Accessed here: https://www.ncronline.org/news/people/dorothy-day-we-are-not-going-subject-birth-control-all-matter-fact.
9. Berkley was married over eight times in his life. Dorothy wrote about him very little.
10. From William D. Miller's 1975 interview with Dorothy Day on Staten Island. Recounted in his book and also in this piece from the *Catholic Worker* newspaper. Bowers, Paul. "An Introduction to *The Eleventh Virgin*." *Catholic Worker*. 2021. https://www.catholicworker.org/pages/eleventh-virgin-intro.html.

A Conversion of Joy

1. Day, *Long Loneliness*, 113.
2. Day, *Long Loneliness*, 132.
3. Day, *Long Loneliness*, 116.
4. Day, *Long Loneliness*, 172.

The Miracle of Love

1. It is interesting to note the privilege Dorothy was able to have in deciding to live in Mexico, with no mention of visas or if she lived there undocumented or not.
2. Day, Dorothy. "Guadalupe." *Commonweal.* February 26, 1930. Accessed here: https://www.commonwealmagazine.org/guadalupe.
3. Day, Dorothy. "Having a Baby." *Catholic Worker*, reprinted in December 1977. Accessed here: https://www.catholicworker.org/dorothyday/articles/583.pdf.
4. In 1977, the *Catholic Worker* reprinted her original essay, with a short intro by Dorothy. She said that in 1929, when she was in Mexico City with Tamar, she met up with Diego Rivera (painter and husband of Frida Kahlo), who took one look at Tamar (then three years old) and said, "I know this little girl." He told Dorothy her article had been reprinted all over the Soviet Union, and she should go there and collect royalties.

The Miracle of Mary

1. For more information on these historic tenement buildings, check out the Tenement Museum in New York City.
2. Day, Dorothy. "Real Revolutionists." *Commonweal.* January 11, 1933. Accessed here: https://www.commonwealmagazine.org/real-revolutionists.
3. Day, Dorothy. "Hunger Marches in Washington." *Commonweal,* vol 48. December 1932. Accessed here: https://www.catholic worker.org/dorothyday/articles/39.pdf. This article was also repurposed for the introduction to *House of Hospitality*, her first book looking back at the origins of the Catholic Worker Movement.
4. Day, *Long Loneliness*, 165.
5. Day, *Long Loneliness*, 165.
6. Day, Dorothy. *House of Hospitality* (Huntington, IN: Our Sunday Visitor Publishing Division, 2015, Seventy-fifth anniversary edition; Originally published 1939), 28.
7. It wasn't a basilica yet in 1932, as construction had halted due to the Great Depression.

Part 2 The Birth of the Catholic Worker

Meeting Peter Maurin

1. Catholic Church. Pope (1878–1903: Leo XIII). Rerum Novarum, *Encyclical Letter on the Condition of the Working Classes* (1891). https://www.vatican.va/content/leo-xiii/en/encyclicals /documents/hf_l-xiii_enc_15051891_rerum-novarum.html; Catholic Church. Pope (1922–1939: Pius XI). Quadragesimo Anno, *Encyclical Letter on Restructuring the Social Order.* Full text accessed here: https://www.vatican.va/content/pius-xi/en /encyclicals/documents/hf_p-xi_enc_19310515_quadragesimo -anno.html.
2. The homesteading partner was male, and his death spurred Peter to become an itinerant traveler. There is no mention of romantic partners that Peter ever put forth publicly. Peter didn't like to talk about his past very much, and all Dorothy could get out of him was that for some years he lived in ways that "were not in keeping with the teachings of the church."
3. Maurin, Peter, and Lincoln Rice. *The Forgotten Radical Peter Maurin: Easy Essays from the Catholic Worker* (New York: Fordham University Press, 2020), 105.

A Little Red Notebook, a Little Stick of Dynamite

1. Piehl, Mel, Dorothy Day, and Peter Maurin. *Breaking Bread* (Philadelphia: Temple University Press, 1982), 8.
2. Day, *House of Hospitality.*

May Day

1. The visual of the front page is just so wonderful. Day, Dorothy. *Catholic Worker* (May 1, 1933). Accessed here: https://merton. bellarmine.edu/files/original/daf15f7742b73d731d7106fb93 e137ec1f259e47.pdf.
2. This is a mangled line from the Joe Hill IWW protest song "The Preacher and the Slave," which says, "You will eat, bye and bye, in

that glorious land above the sky, work and pray, live on hay, you'll get pie in the sky when you die."

3. Day, *House of Hospitality*, 42.

Good as Bread

1. Day, *House of Hospitality,* 39.
2. Day, Dorothy. *Loaves and Fishes* (San Fransisco: Harper and Row, 1965), 9.
3. Thank you to Loughery and Randolph for so succinctly summing up these philosophies on page 138.

How Prayer Works

1. This phrase is attributed to base ecclesial communities and liberation theologians.
2. See Matthew 25 and the story of the sheep and the goats.
3. Statistics directly from the *Catholic Worker*, Day, Dorothy. "Must Evictions Continue? Sign Pledge in Opposition." *Catholic Worker*. November, 1933, 4. Accessed here: https://merton.bellarmine.edu/files/original/de1d82df5caf3a1ae57 60090719c5fa1ff397218.pdf.
4. At the time, it was called "the largest bedroom in the world," and it was in Dorothy's backyard, so to speak (*House of Hospitality*, 68).
5. Day, *House of Hospitality*, 45.
6. Day, Dorothy. "House of Hospitality." *Catholic Worker*. May 1939. Accessed here: https://www.catholicworker.org/dorothyday /articles/342.pdf.
7. Maurin, Peter. "To the Bishops of the U.S.: A Plea for Houses of Hospitality." *Catholic Worker*. October 1933, 1. Accessed here: https://merton.bellarmine.edu/files/original/eedd828204e58ffc 6ae45ace37a95f022dda748b.pdf.
8. Day, *House of Hospitality*, 60.
9. Day, Dorothy. "Co-operative Apartment for Unemployed Women Has Its Start in Parish." *Catholic Worker*. December 1933, 1. Accessed here: https://merton.bellarmine.edu/files/original /e9f94453391b9bc99f3649e36d97aa9489566152.pdf.

NOTES

10. Lincoln Rice mentions this story in his book on Peter Maurin, as does Jim Forest, but Dorothy never talked about it publicly.
11. Frias, Laura. "The Average Minimum Wage Worker Has to Work More than Two Full Time Jobs in Order to Afford a Two Bedroom Rental Anywhere in the US." *Insider.* July 2020. Accessed here: https://www.businessinsider.com/full-time-minimum-wage-workers-cant-afford-rent-anywhere-us-2020-7.

The Paper Grows, and So Does the House

1. Ellul, Jacques, and Geoffrey Bromiley. *Anarchy and Christianity* (Eugene, OR: Wipf & Stock, 2011), 13.
2. Ellul and Bromiley, *Anarchy and Christianity*, 14.
3. Day, Dorothy. "On Pilgrimage: November 1956." *Catholic Worker.* November, 1956. Accessed here: https://www.catholicworker.org/dorothyday/articles/714.html.
4. Day, "On Pilgrimage."
5. In reading about these early houses, one can quickly grasp the issues with putting no parameters on behavior. While it sounds beautiful in practice, it is inherently exclusionary. For example, in the 1930s, anti-Black racism and anti-Semitism were rampant among the people who showed up on Mott Street to grab some coffee and bread. This never made it into her plucky columns, but oftentimes white men in line would refuse to allow Black men to stand in line next to them to receive coffee. What was an anarchist, pacifist, Catholic house of mercy to do? They simply served everyone who showed and tried to address these issues in their papers and through community meetings in order to change hearts and minds.
6. Day, Dorothy. "And Now, a Note of Melancholy." *Catholic Worker.* November 1933, 4. Accessed here: https://merton.bellarmine.edu/files/original/de1d82df5caf3a1ae5760090719c5fa1ff397218.pdf.
7. Day, Dorothy, and Robert Ellsberg. *The Duty of Delight: The Diaries of Dorothy Day* (New York: Image Books, 2011).

Love in Action

1. Day and Ellsberg, *The Duty of Delight*, 5.

252

2. Day and Ellsberg, *Duty of Delight*, 11.
3. Riegle, Rosalie. *Dorothy Day: Portrait by Those Who Knew Her* (Ossining, NY: Orbis Books, 2006), 151.
4. Day, *Loaves and Fishes*, 24.
5. Macdonald, Dwight. "The Foolish Things of the World." *The New Yorker*. September 27, 1952. https://www.newyorker.com /magazine/1952/10/04/the-foolish-things-of-the-world.
6. Day, *Loaves and Fishes*, 30.
7. Day, *Loaves and Fishes*, 38.
8. Loughery and Randolph, *Dorothy Day*, 170.

Part 3 The Work Continues

The Duty of Delight

1. Her granddaughter, Kate Hennesy, titled her book on her mother and grandmother after this exact quote because of its importance to Dorothy.

Just Sitting Around Talking

1. Riegle, *Dorothy Day: Portraits*, 30.
2. Day, *Loaves and Fishes*, 39.
3. Day and Ellsberg, *Duty of Delight*, 14.
4. Day, Dorothy. "Technique of Agitation." *Catholic Worker*. December 1933, 2. Accessed here: https://merton.bellarmine .edu/files/original/e9f94453391b9bc99f3649e36d97aa948956 6152.pdf.
5. I am indebted to Brian Terrell and his observations about Dorothy's faith in the context of the Worker.
6. By some accounts, Dwight MacDonald fell in love with Dorothy just like everyone else did—to the point where he even let her review and edit the profile he wrote on her. The editors of the *New Yorker* would have been highly displeased by this, and onlookers recall Dorothy sitting at her kitchen table and crossing out entire sentences in the profile, editing her life story like she always did. Lougherty and Randolph, *Dorothy Day: Dissenting Voice*, 258.
7. Day, *Long Loneliness*, 286.

Mother of a Movement

1. Riegle, *Dorothy Day: Portraits*, 1.
2. Loughery and Randolph, *Dorothy Day*, 171.
3. Hennessy, Kate. *Dorothy Day: The World Will Be Saved by Beauty* (New York: Scribner, 2017), 82.
4. While Tamar speaks positively of her time at the Worker, she was the only child to live long term in one of the houses of hospitality. The safety of children and other vulnerable people was not mentioned much in Dorothy's writings, but she actively discouraged against families or people with children embarking on such an endeavor. Perhaps she knew an anarchist leaning in these regards meant it was very hard to safeguard against abuse.
5. Riegle, *Dorothy Day: Portraits*, 109.
6. Accessed here: https://www.bc.edu/content/dam/files/centers /boisi/pdf/S17/Hennessy%20final.pdf.
7. Riegle, *Dorothy Day: Portraits*, 110.

The Mystical, Mythical Body of Christ

1. Day, Dorothy. "There Is No Negro Problem! There Is an Interracial Problem Which Concerns Every One of Us." *Catholic Worker*. January, 1937, 8. Accessed here: https://merton.bellar mine.edu/files/original/4b1914e3eff4c0b918a227f901541c1e 0e6879bd.pdf.
2. Rice, Lincoln. "The Catholic Worker Movement and Racial Justice: A Precarious Relationship." *Horizons* 46, no. 1 (2019): 55. https:// doi.org/10.1017/hor.2019.9.
3. Galations 3:28.
4. Rice, Lincoln. *Healing the Racial Divide: A Catholic Racial Justice Framework Inspired by Dr. Arthur Falls* (Eugene, OR: Pickwick Publications, 2014), 48.
5. For more information on this wonderful man, I recommend reading Lincoln Rice's book *Healing the Racial Divide*.
6. Day, Dorothy. "On Pilgrimage March–April 1970." *Catholic Worker*. April 1970. Accessed here: https://www.catholicworker .org/dorothyday/articles/499.pdf.

War and Violence

1. Day, Dorothy. "Grave Injustice Done Japanese on West Coast." *Catholic Worker*. June 1943. Accessed here: https://www.catholicworker.org/dorothyday/articles/218.pdf.
2. No, the irony of the name of the paper is not lost on me.
3. They did not listen to him, refusing to resettle the majority of asylum seekers.
4. Accessed here: https://archive.org/details/DorothyDay/page/n9/mode/2up?_ga=2.21996536.298433258.1615842383-1388701595.1611433251.
5. Day, Dorothy. "Pacifism." *Catholic Worker*. May 1936. Accessed here: https://www.catholicworker.org/dorothyday/articles/215.html.

A Conversion of Piety

1. Day, Dorothy. "Aims and Purposes." *Catholic Worker*. February 1940, 7. Accessed here: https://www.catholicworker.org/dorothyday/articles/182.html.
2. Hennessy, *Dorothy Day: The World Will Be Saved by Beauty*, 128.

All the Ways to Be a Saint

1. Otterman, Sharon. "In Hero of the Catholic Left, a Conservative Cardinal Sees a Saint." *The New York Times*. November 2012. Accessed here: https://www.nytimes.com/2012/11/27/nyregion/sainthood-for-dorothy-day-has-unexpected-champion-in-cardinal-timothy-dolan.html.
2. Gibson, David. "St. Dorothy? Controversial, Yes, but Bishops Push for Canonization." *Religion News Services*. November 2012. Accessed here: https://www.ncronline.org/news/spirituality/st-dorothy-day-controversial-yes-bishops-push-canonization.
3. "USCCB General Assembly—2012." United States Conference of Catholic Bishops video on-demand, 42:00. https://www.usccb.org/offices/general-secretariat/usccb-general-assembly-2012-november-video-demand.

4. Time Inc. "Religion: The Poor Man." *Time*. May 30, 1949. Accessed here: http://content.time.com/time/subscriber/article /0,33009,888007,00.html.
5. This is obviously not normal, nor exactly ethical, journalistic practice, but Michael Harrington relayed that the author Dwight MacDonald fell in love with Dorothy, allowing her to strike out lines from the profile, including references to her drinking gangsters under the table (Loughlin and Rudolph, 258).

Afterword: The Story of a Movement, the Story of Hunger

1. Gustavo, Gutiérrez. *The God of Life* (Ossining, NY: Orbis Books, 1996), xiii.
2. I highly recommend reading the new edited volumes on her writing from the 1970s and '60s, edited by Robert Ellsberg.
3. Archer, Kristjan, and Justin Mccarthy. "US Catholics Have Backed Same-Sex Marriage since 2011." *Gallup*. October 2020. Accessed here: https://news.gallup.com/poll/322805/catholics-backed -sex-marriage-2011.aspx.